Setting the Scene for Positive Behaviour in the Early Years

Disruptive behaviour can pose a challenge to any early years practitioner in childcare and early education settings. Various strategies exist for dealing with such behaviour, but very often these rely on the labelling of the child as a 'problem', with all the negative connotations that this implies. This book is aimed at anyone who works with young children and wishes to ensure that the strategies they use when intervening in their behaviour are as positive as possible. Throughout, the focus is on positive changes that setting staff can make to maximise positive behaviour. The children are not labelled, but enabled.

Based on his vast experience in the field, the author provides here an array of positive behaviour strategies that can be successful with the widest variety of children, whatever the 'reason' for their behaviour. Specifically designed to be accessible to all early years practitioners, this book includes strategies and advice on:

◆ How to structure learning environments to encourage positive behaviour
◆ Providing equality of opportunity, and responding to individual needs
◆ Teaching emotional literacy
◆ Working in partnership with parents
◆ Positive strategies for working with children with particular difficulties

Case studies are frequently used to illustrate good practice, and practitioners will find within a wealth of tried and tested strategies that have resulted in real improvements to young children's behaviour.

Essential reading for teachers and early years workers at any setting, in addition to students studying childcare at NVQ or degree level, this book will be of real value to anyone who cares about young children's behaviour and wishes to make their earliest experiences of the education system as positive as possible.

Having previously worked as a teacher and educational psychologist in inner London, **Jason Swale** is currently Senior Early Years Area Inclusion Co-ordinator in Tower Hamlets. His research interests include parental partnership in education and young children's emotional development.

Setting the Scene for Positive Behaviour in the Early Years

A framework for good practice

Jason Swale

Routledge
Taylor & Francis Group

LONDON AND NEW YORK

First published 2006 by Routledge
2 Park Square, Milton Park
Abingdon, Oxon OX14 4RN

Simultaneously published in the USA and Canada
by Routledge
270 Madison Ave, New York, NY 10016

Routledge is an imprint of the Taylor & Francis Group

© 2006 Jason Swale

Typeset in Times New Roman by
Florence Production Ltd, Stoodleigh, Devon
Printed and bound in Great Britain by
Bell & Bain Ltd, Glasgow

British Library Cataloguing in Publication Data
A catalogue record for this book is available from the
British Library

Library of Congress Cataloging in Publication Data
Swale, Jason, 1967–
   Setting the scene for positive behaviour in the early years: a framework
   for good practice/Jason Swale.
       p. cm.
     Includes bibliographical references and index.
   1. Behaviour modification.   2. Socialization – Study and teaching
   (early childhood)   I. Title
   LB1060.2.S88 2006
   370.15′28 – dc22   2005024065

ISBN 10: 0–415–37312–3

ISBN 13: 9–78–0–415–37312–8

Contents

Acknowledgements

I would like to thank the many people who have contributed in some way to this book. Firstly, I am indebted to all the early years practitioners who have inspired and motivated me in my work, and who continue to do so. Many of the ideas in this book have been inspired by the excellent practice that I regularly see in settings.

I must also thank the children with whom I have had the pleasure to work, as they have taught me everything I know about their behaviour! When trying out new ideas about what I thought might work well, they soon let me know if I was on the right track. Thanks are also due to their parents for helping me to understand what true partnership means.

Thank you also to my colleagues for reviewing my proposal, sharing their thoughts and expertise, and for proofreading chapter drafts and making insightful comments. A particular thank you to Anne Savill for her input on children's anger, and to Cesia Prytys, for helping me get started.

Thank you too, to all the people at Routledge who have been involved in the many stages of preparing this book.

Finally, thank you to Rich, for his confidence in me, to Sú Sì, just for being there, and to my Mum for shaping who I am today in ways I am only just beginning to appreciate.

Introduction

In recent years, reports in the media and anecdotal evidence from those working in childcare and education in the UK suggest that there has been an alarming growth in the number of children displaying what is variously called 'problem behaviour', 'challenging behaviour' or, simply, 'bad behaviour'. Tabloid newspapers have labelled even very young children as 'monsters', 'feral' or 'thugs'. Exclusions from schools have increased significantly over the past years, and, more recently, there have been reports of children as young as 3 and 4 being excluded from their nursery, playgroup or school, with the reason given invariably linked to the child's behaviour.

Various explanations are put forward for this apparent deterioration in the behaviour of our children. The behaviour of some children is attributed to conditions such as Attention Deficit Hyperactivity Disorder (ADHD), autism or 'conduct disorder', while for others, the explanation given is linked to the child's environment. This is particularly the case in less affluent, urban areas where there may be limited opportunities for children to play outside safely and few opportunities for leisure and recreational activities. Parents are very often blamed for their children's behaviour, with reasons given varying from the parent working too many hours or failing to set boundaries, to over-indulging the child. When marital or partnership relationships break down, at what is a very difficult time for parents, they sometimes have the additional burden of guilt, feeling that their children will suffer as a result. Single mothers have been demonised by both press and politicians, with the whole nation's ills put at their door. Interestingly, single fathers with sole parental responsibility have not suffered the same fate, instead being lauded almost as heroes.

People working in education and childcare are now often asked: 'How do you manage?' Children's behaviour is increasingly seen as unmanageable, which in some cases has become a self-fulfilling prophecy. In certain areas, and for certain groups of children, low expectations have undoubtedly led to a deterioration in both achievement and behaviour. Yet it need not be that way. While the above 'reasons' may all in certain circumstances impact upon a child's behaviour, those people who work with the child are not – or should not be – passive individuals who have no influence over a child's behaviour. Why is it that two nurseries, playgroups or schools in the same area, and with similar intake, can be so different? One may have an excellent reputation, while the other might be described as a failing setting. The answer probably lies in the ethos, organisation and staffing of the setting, and the support that it gives to its children. Of course, it is likely that there will always be a small number of children who display behaviour that challenges practitioners, in some cases significantly so. However, the way in which the setting is organised, its beliefs and the way its staff respond to such behaviour will to a large extent determine the outcomes for these children and, ultimately, the success of the setting as a whole. Education settings are increasingly expected to be inclusive – welcoming to all children and families, regardless of factors such as disability, ethnicity, culture or class. However, children whose behaviour challenges us are among the most difficult to successfully include, which highlights the importance of positive strategies to support positive behaviour. In turn, positive behaviour leads to true inclusion.

While many books about children's behaviour focus on the child as the 'problem', this book takes a different approach. The main focus is environmental and systemic. As the title suggests, the aim is to provide *positive* behaviour strategies, and ones that can be successful with the widest variety of children, whatever the 'reason' for their behaviour. Of course, it can be very useful to know, or to make an informed guess at, the reason why a child behaves as they do. But at times it may be more useful to focus less on the 'reason', and more on what can be done to bring about positive changes in behaviour. Of course, interventions are informed by knowledge of individual children and their circumstances, but sometimes we may be misinformed, or may misunderstand a child's behaviour. In particular, seeking to blame someone for the child's behaviour – usually the parents or carers – is most often counterproductive. Practitioners are unable to change a child's domestic circumstances, but they can effect enormous change within their own settings. Focusing on what cannot be changed is a negative response to a situation, which will not improve matters for the child or the parent. The 'blame' mentality is also very detrimental to the practitioner, often leading to feelings of depression, powerlessness, ineffectiveness and a hostile, or at best strained, relationship with the child's parents. In contrast, focusing on what *can* be changed within the setting is a positive response, and one that can lead to empowerment, not only for the practitioner but also for the child and parents.

Information on possible within-child 'reasons' for children's behaviour is included where appropriate, but this is never the primary focus of any particular chapter. The main focus will always be upon positive strategies and changes that can be implemented in the setting, usually quite simply and without creating an unmanageable workload for the practitioner. All behaviour can be seen as a form of communication, and the way in which practitioners communicate back to the child can make all the difference. Children's feelings need to be acknowledged, accepted and responded to in an appropriate way. If not, behaviour difficulties are unlikely to improve and may well deteriorate further.

When thinking about children's behaviour, it is 'difficult' behaviour that most often springs to mind. However, it is important to remember that children who are withdrawn, distressed or emotionally disturbed are also in need of support and positive intervention. Such children are easily overlooked – particularly the quieter ones – in hectic environments where the children displaying disruptive and attention-seeking behaviour tend to take up the majority of practitioners' time. For this reason, this book will also consider the needs of withdrawn and distressed children, and how these can be addressed through positive intervention on the part of the practitioner.

This book focuses in particular on children in their early years, which in this context covers the age range 3 to 5. Many of the strategies in the book can be used successfully with older or younger children, but the case studies relate to children in playgroups (sometimes called pre-schools), day nurseries, children's centres, nursery schools and nursery and reception classes in primary schools. The word *setting* is used throughout the book, in recognition of the fact that practitioners in the private and voluntary sectors are often overlooked, and much of the existing literature uses the terminology of maintained schools. The word *parents* is used throughout as shorthand to stand for the diversity of arrangements for looking after and bringing up children in contemporary Britain. Children may be described as *she*, *he* or *they* in recognition of the fact that all behaviours are common to both girls and boys.

It is hoped that this book will be a useful resource to all practitioners working in the early years, and that it will help them to give a positive response when asked: 'How do you manage?' The book is intended to be used flexibly and does not necessarily need to be read sequentially. Practitioners should feel free to dip into it as they wish, making use of what they find useful. It is hoped that the book will also inspire practitioners to develop their own creative solutions and strategies to encourage positive behaviour.

In an increasingly challenging and complex world, we owe it to our children to provide them with the best possible care and education. In order to do so, we need to have the highest expectations not only of their academic abilities but also their behaviour. By 'setting the scene' for positive behaviour, we give all children the best possible chance to succeed in their early education setting and throughout their lives to come.

Chapter 1

A positive start

The importance of preparation

For children – and their parents – starting in the first setting, or in a new setting, is an event of major significance in their lives. The value of careful planning and preparation cannot be underestimated. Some children will remember their first days into adulthood, so it makes sense to make these memories as positive as possible. A negative start to childcare or early education can impact upon a child's development and success throughout their future education. Young children can be labelled as 'naughty' in their first few days in a setting, and this label is easily passed from practitioner to practitioner, so that expectations can be established even before a particular adult has met the child in question.

Labels such as 'naughty' are invariably linked to low expectations, not only of behaviour, but also of academic achievement. Thus the label 'naughty' can potentially condemn a child to a childhood characterised by underachievement and low self-esteem. Ultimately, a child who underachieves and has low self-esteem is more likely to grow up to be an adult who underachieves and has low self-esteem. Early years practitioners, therefore, have a tremendous responsibility towards new children, to ensure that their early experiences are positive ones, which make them feel welcome, secure and successful. So, what needs to be done?

There are two main stages involved in planning and preparation for a new child. These are **information gathering** and **making arrangements for settling-in**.

Information gathering

Occasionally, a child will start unexpectedly in a setting, perhaps having just moved into the area. However, in the majority of cases, an application will have been made to the setting some time before the child's start date. All settings have application forms, but these can vary greatly in the information they ask for. Apart from the basics such as name, address, telephone number and date of birth, many will ask additional questions. For example, a common question is 'Does your child have special educational needs?', and this information is often used to prioritise places. While this is a valid question, parents should not be expected to go into minute detail on the application form. Questions such as 'Does your child have behaviour problems?' are to be avoided. Parents may feel (justifiably, in some cases) that if they say 'yes' to such a question, they may not be offered a place in the setting. Accordingly, many parents choose not to disclose behaviour issues on an application form.

As a rule of thumb, the form should ask for just enough information to enable the setting to offer places according to fair and transparent criteria. Once places have been offered and accepted, more detailed information about children – including their behaviour where applicable – can be gathered during a face-to-face meeting with parents. The following information should be gathered, ideally during a home or setting visit prior to the child's start date.

◆ significant early experiences
◆ the child's strengths
◆ the child's likes and dislikes (including food and drink)
◆ any fears or phobias a child may have
◆ any allergies, medical conditions or concerns
◆ whether the parent feels the child needs additional help or support in any particular area
◆ strategies parents use when they feel challenged by their child's behaviour.

All of the above can have a profound effect upon both the child's behaviour and their achievement in the setting, so it makes sense for practitioners to be aware of these things right from the start. This information needs to be shared between *all* the practitioners who come into contact with the child, not just the child's keyworker. It may be a good idea to hold a staff meeting where all members of staff have an opportunity to go through the paperwork for each child, taking note of significant information and its implications.

Significant early experiences

Finding out about these experiences may help the practitioner to understand why children behave as they do, but as stated in the Introduction, practitioners should not get too caught up in debating the 'reasons' for a child's behaviour at the expense of planning positive steps to improve matters. *Case study: Besnik* illustrates how information about a child's early experiences was used to inform practice in a Nursery class.

The child's strengths

Information on the child's strengths should always be sought before discussing any difficulties. If parents are asked first to focus on positive aspects of their child's development, they are likely to find it easier to then discuss any areas of difficulty or concern. If the focus becomes entrenched in the child's difficulties, the practitioner will be able to remind parents of a child's strengths, thus shifting the focus back onto more positive aspects of the child. It can also be helpful for practitioners to be reminded of a child's strengths at times when they are faced with particularly 'difficult' behaviour.

Case study: Besnik

Besnik, aged 4, and his parents turned up unexpectedly at an inner-city primary school, accompanied by a social worker. The family were refugees, who had recently arrived from Kosovo, having fled the conflict in their country. As there was a place in the Nursery class, the headteacher, in consultation with the Nursery class teacher, agreed that Besnik could start in the class the following day. The school had a positive policy of arranging half an hour of emergency supply cover for teachers in such cases, to allow the teacher to meet with parents to gather important information.

Ideally, the school liked to arrange an interpreter for meetings with parents whose English was not yet fluent. However, in this case, it was too short notice to arrange an Albanian interpreter for the meeting. Besnik's parents managed, however, to convey something of the horror and destruction the family had witnessed in Kosovo in the weeks before they left. In particular, they warned, Besnik was terrified of loud noises, having experienced both machine-gun fire, and grenades, one of which had badly damaged the family home.

In response to this information, the Nursery staff decided to ban balloons from the Nursery for the time being (balloons were often used as part of physical play activities) to avoid Besnik becoming distressed if a balloon burst. To begin to desensitise Besnik to loud noises, staff planned a series of percussion sessions. The children were given various percussion instruments, including triangles, shakers, tambourines and small drums. Besnik, to his delight, was given the largest drum. The group began by playing their instruments very quietly, and built up over three sessions to playing them loudly. This progression meant that Besnik was not shocked by the loud noise, and as he was the one beating the drum, he had complete control over the volume of the noise he made. Besnik quickly learnt to love playing the drum. Although he continued to be startled by loud, unexpected noises for some time (which staff took pains to minimise), he no longer cried or withdrew to a corner when he heard them, and quickly returned to his play.

The child's likes and dislikes

Gathering information about the child's likes and dislikes is also very important. This information helps the practitioner to plan appropriate activities and experiences for the child to make starting in the setting as positive an experience as possible. If children are offered familiar and favourite activities when they arrive, they are far less likely to be distressed or overwhelmed by the new environment. Familiar activities will also encourage communication between the child and practitioner ('I've got one of those at home!') and be a good starting point for the development of a secure adult–child relationship. Of course, new and novel experiences and activities should also be available for more adventurous children, and to encourage challenge and risk-taking.

Activities and equipment should reflect a wide range of cultural backgrounds (e.g. balti dishes, woks and chopsticks in the role-play area; multicultural dressing-up clothes). Again, these familiar items will help the child to feel secure in their new environment. They also give a very powerful message to the child – that his or her culture is recognised and respected. This in itself will promote the child's self-esteem, and thus lay the foundations for positive behaviour.

Where possible, in the child's first few days in the setting, it is a good idea to avoid things that parents have identified as definite 'dislikes' for the child. It is, of course, perfectly acceptable to offer a 'disliked' activity (e.g. a messy activity) as one of a *range* of activities from which the child may choose (what is a disliked activity for one child may be a favourite for another). However, a child should not be expected to join in with a 'disliked' activity at this stage.

It is particularly important to ensure that the child's first experiences of lunchtimes are as positive as possible. For some children, this may be the first time they have eaten a meal outside of the family home. There should be a range of food available so that children can avoid those things they dislike. Of course, at a later stage, practitioners will want to encourage children to try new things, or even to retry something described as 'yucky'. However, the best time to do this is probably not during the child's first few days in the setting. An alarming number of children are developing eating disorders, previously thought of as exclusively adult conditions. Food and eating can arouse powerful emotions even in very young children, and it is vital that these are positive emotions in order to minimise the possibility of difficulties developing at a later stage. Lunchtimes and snacktimes are discussed in more detail in Chapter 2.

Fears and phobias

In the same way that it is important to take account of the child's likes and dislikes, it is also important to give careful consideration to any fears or phobias a child may have. This is well illustrated in the case study earlier in this chapter. To give another example, if a child is terrified of the dark, it would probably not be a good idea to turn the setting's role-play area into a 'haunted house' during the first half term.

Allergies, medical conditions and concerns

This information is clearly vital. Certain food allergies, for example, can trigger hyperactivity, which may lead to behaviour that could be misunderstood as 'naughtiness' if the adult were unaware of the allergy. A child may have a particular medical diagnosis that impacts upon their behaviour, such as Asperger's Syndrome, dyspraxia or ADHD. If a child has a medical diagnosis, practitioners should take steps to learn as much as possible about their condition and how it may affect their behaviour. A child's parents usually have a wealth of information on their child's condition and strategies they use to manage its effects. Talking to parents is a useful first step towards understanding the child's condition. More information on working with such children is found in Chapter 8.

In the absence of any identified condition or diagnosis, a parent may still have concerns over their child's health or physical condition. Such concerns should be taken very seriously, as parents know their child best. Even if a practitioner feels that parents' concerns are unfounded, it is important that their views are respected and their advice borne in mind. Many medical conditions may remain undiagnosed until a child has started in an early years setting. Practitioners and parents are in a far better position to notice patterns of behaviour than medical professionals who are often expected to carry out a single assessment of the child in an unfamiliar context and environment. In many cases, the parent will not yet have consulted their GP. Sometimes parents want to 'wait and see' until the child starts pre-school or nursery, and in such cases parents will be anxious to hear your views. In most cases, it is important that you give a child at least a term to settle into the setting before sharing your views with parents. Even then, it is not the practitioner's role to speculate on medical diagnoses. However, if parents and practitioners alike share significant concerns, this is a sign that outside support should be sought. In the meantime, however, practitioners should focus upon the positive strategies described in this book to encourage positive behaviour, and not become unduly focused on medical labels.

Additional help or support

If a parent feels that their child needs additional help or support in any particular area, or if this has been advised by a professional who knows the child, the early years practitioner should incorporate this into their planning right from the start. If a child significantly struggles in any area, and is unsupported, this is likely to be a very negative experience for them, which may have a detrimental effect upon their enjoyment of the setting in general. At the very least, the child is likely to feel that the activity with which they struggle is unpleasant, or not worth doing. Such feelings can have a devastating effect upon the child's achievement and behaviour, not just in the early years, but throughout their subsequent education and life.

Of course, it may be that the child exceeds the parent's expectations, and does not in fact need this additional help in the setting. What children are able to do at home, and what they are able to do in an early years setting may differ. Sometimes watching other children do something provides the impetus for a child to try something they thought they could not do, and to persevere with something they find difficult. Apparent difficulties may simply be due to a child having had limited opportunities to practice certain skills. For example, on weekday mornings a busy parent who has three children to drop at school before rushing to work is unlikely to have time to allow her 3-year-old to practise dressing skills. In a setting however, the child has much more time to get to grips with the complexities of buttons, and trousers that turn themselves inside out. It should also be remembered that children can be very skilful at getting their parents to do things for them that they can in fact do for themselves! If the child is given additional help or support that they turn out not to need, no harm has been done. However, if the child is not offered this support, and does need it, damage can quickly be done.

It is important that the practitioner is honest with the parent about the level of support that can be offered. If a parent expresses the view that their child will need a significant amount of one-to-one support, the practitioner will need to explain exactly how much the staff in the setting can offer.[1] It should also be pointed out that children often learn better when supported in a small group than when having an adult by their side all day long. Even at this age, children are very adept at noticing differences between themselves and their peers. If the other children in the setting spend most of their time in self-directed activity, the one-to-one supported child may quickly learn to feel 'different', which may lead to self-consciousness, resentment or 'acting out'.

Strategies used by parents

It is very useful to gather information on the strategies parents themselves use when they feel challenged by their child's behaviour. It is helpful to find out both about strategies that have worked well, and those that have been less successful.

Strategies that have worked well at home can be implemented in the setting, provided that they are not punitive or otherwise inappropriate. If the practitioner does feel that a strategy is inappropriate, s/he needs to be sensitive to the parent's views and explain why such a strategy would not be used in the setting. The most obvious example is that of smacking. If a parent says that she smacks her child, and asks if this strategy could be used in the setting, the practitioner could explain that it is illegal to do so. This is a simple, factual explanation that avoids entering into a debate over moral issues. If, on the other hand, the practitioner were to respond with: 'We don't smack children in our nursery because it's barbaric and violates the rights of the child', this comment would be very likely to offend or demean the parent. The parent is likely to feel defensive, and that her parenting skills are being called into question. The end result will be a strained relationship between parent and practitioner, in which the parent decides not to share any further information with the setting for fear of being negatively judged. Clearly, this scenario is in the interests of neither the setting, the parents nor the child.

As all those who work with young children know, their behaviour at home and in nursery or pre-school can be very different. For this reason, the practitioner may wish to try strategies that have not been successful in the home. If such strategies are found to work in the setting, practitioners will again need to be sensitive to parents' feelings when sharing this information. It is important that parents are not made to feel inadequate or that they were doing something 'wrong'. It is often helpful to reiterate to parents just how differently children can behave in nursery to at home. If appropriate, where practitioners have children of their own, they could even share their own experiences of this phenomenon to reassure parents that they are not alone.

---

1 For a very small number of children, significant levels of one-to-one support may be necessary. This is likely to be the case for children with severe learning difficulties and/or physical difficulties or profound sensory impairment in mainstream settings. However, in these cases, statutory assessment is likely to have been completed and the additional support should already have been arranged. Careful planning and preparation is vital to allow children with complex needs a positive start to their early years education. The setting, along with the local authority, has a responsibility to ensure that adequate arrangements are in place *before* the child starts in the setting.

Practitioners should let parents know exactly how a strategy was implemented, as it may be that the parents can slightly adjust what they were doing at home to good effect. Parents should be reminded of the importance of *consistency* in implementing a strategy. However, they should know that if a strategy is unsuccessful after having been tried for a reasonable period of time, something new should be tried. If the parent asks for the practitioner's advice on strategies, the practitioner should share things that have worked well for them, while stressing that what works well for one child may not necessarily be successful for another.

How to gather the information

Wherever possible, it is strongly recommended that practitioners find time to meet with parents and their child before the child's start date in order to gather the relevant information. If for any reason this is not possible, the information should be collected as soon as possible after the child has started in the setting.

Home visiting

An increasing number of early years practitioners in both pre-school settings and schools are visiting children and their parents at home before the child's formal entry into the setting. There are arguments both for and against home visiting, but the majority of practitioners who have introduced such visits have found them to be invaluable. Well planned and high quality home visits provide an opportunity to meet with parents and children in an environment in which they are comfortable. It is of course vital that parents are made aware that a home visit is optional, and that they may choose to meet with staff in the setting if they prefer.

The first question for practitioners who have never visited children at home may well be: 'When do we find the time to do home visits?' There are many different arrangements in place for home visiting and settings will need to decide what will work best for them. Where the majority of children tend to start in the setting at the same time of year, it may be possible to open the setting (or early years unit within a school) a few days later than the usual start of term in order to provide time for home visiting. Provided that they are made aware of the benefits of home visits, headteachers in schools, governors and management committees in non-maintained settings will often give permission for this arrangement to be made. Alternatively, staff may visit children at home at the end of the setting day in the term preceding their entry, but this is only really feasible for one or two children per day. The third option, where staffing ratios allow, is for practitioners to visit new children during the setting day. Whatever arrangement is made, it is prudent for two staff to visit a child's home, to carry a mobile phone and to let other staff know the times and addresses of their visits.

When offering home visits to parents, practitioners should make the purpose of the visit clear, and try to allay any fears parents might have about staff 'checking up on them' or making negative judgements about their home or living arrangements. Practitioners should try to be as flexible as possible with the times they offer, so that working parents do not have to take time off work in order to meet with them in their home. As already stated, parents must feel able to decline the offer of a home visit, and should not feel that they are inconveniencing staff or being uncooperative by doing so. There are many possible reasons why parents might not wish to be visited at home, and practitioners should not draw any conclusions from such a decision. Instead, a visit should be arranged in the setting, at a time convenient to the parents, during which the necessary information can be collected.

Home visits should be started fairly informally, with the practitioners taking the lead from the parents, who may wish to ask particular questions, or from the child, who may wish to show them a favourite toy. If the staff have made an introductory photo book about their setting (which is strongly recommended), this can be shown to the child. Such a book will help to familiarise the child with the setting, and can include information about routines and rules so that the child knows what to expect. Similarly, some settings have made a video about their provision, and this can be shown during a home visit or loaned to parents to watch in their own time. Some practitioners take photographs of children during the home visit, which are then on display as children arrive on their first day, helping them to make a connection between home and setting and to feel welcome.

Practitioners should try not to refuse parents' hospitality if offered a drink or other light refreshments during a home visit. Accepting this hospitality can be a good ice-breaker and may be an important part of welcoming someone into the family home in some cultures. Once both practitioners and parents feel comfortable, the information listed in the first section of this chapter can be gathered.

Meeting in the setting

If a home visit is not possible or unwanted by parents, a meeting in the setting can follow much the same format as a home visit. The main difference is that parents (and the child if present) are on the practitioners' 'territory' rather than their own, and practitioners should make every effort to make them feel welcome and relaxed. For example, refreshments can be offered and staff could start the visit with an informal guided tour of the setting.

Information-gathering meetings should ideally be before or after the setting day, when other children and parents are not present. This ensures confidentiality for parents and means that staff will be able to devote their full attention to the meeting. If the child is present at the meeting, appropriate activities that do not need close adult supervision should be provided, as children are likely to become bored during the information-gathering part of the visit. Where children do choose to stay by their parents' side, questions should where appropriate be addressed to them as well as to their parents.

The past few sections of this chapter have highlighted the importance of information gathering as a first and crucial step in preparing for a child's entry to a setting. Once all the relevant information has been collected, arrangements can then be made for children's settling-in to the setting.

Making arrangements for settling-in

Visiting the setting

Ideally, all children and parents should be given the opportunity to visit the setting during one of its sessions in the term preceding entry. To ensure that such visits run smoothly, parents should be made aware, in a positive way, that they are responsible for their child's supervision during the visit. Staff should also make clear how long such visits are expected to last. Obviously, times of transition such as lunchtimes, or days on which there are special events are not good times for visits to the setting.

It is a good idea to prepare the children already attending the setting for such visits. They should be encouraged to greet and welcome the visiting child, and to invite them to play. They should be taught to make allowances for a visiting child if, for example, he snatches a toy. However, they should also know how to seek adult support if they need it. If a visiting child does display some unwanted behaviour, practitioners should deal with it as positively as possible, reassuring the parents that many children act in such a way when in a new environment for the first time. They should be told that their child will quickly learn to behave as wanted when he has started in the setting.

Even if a practitioner has been particularly challenged by a child's behaviour, the visit should always end with her telling the child and parents that she is looking forward to them starting in the setting next term.

Staggering entry

It is strongly recommended that settings stagger their entry so they do not have large numbers of new children all starting on the same day. Staggering the entry over, say, four weeks allows practitioners to give new children individual attention in order to make their starting in the setting as positive an experience as possible. If a new child does display unwanted behaviour, it is far easier to deal with this in a positive way if there are only a few new children needing extra adult attention. Where staff know in advance that a particular child may have some difficulties in behaving as wanted, thought should be given as to when the child should begin in the setting. Depending on the child's needs, it may be best to settle her in a small group before the majority of the children have started. Alternatively, staff may judge that it is better to settle the other children first before she starts in the setting. Of course, staff should not automatically assume there will be difficulties – the child might well defy expectations and settle happily into the setting, behaving as wanted.

Building up to a full session or day

Whether a child has a full-time or part-time place in the setting, it is often a good idea to begin with reduced hours and build up to a full session. Some children will take to the setting immediately, separating from their parents with no difficulty and taking delight in exploring what the setting has to offer. Such children will probably be able to cope with a full session within a matter of days. For some children, starting in the setting may be much more of a challenge (for them, their parents, the staff, or any combination of these). Where children are unduly distressed, or have extreme difficulty behaving as wanted, it may be better to build up to a full session to allow children to adjust to their new environment.

Practitioners should discuss session lengths with parents, making arrangements that are beneficial to the child and acceptable to the parents. Practitioners should not use 'unacceptable behaviour' as an excuse for keeping a child on reduced hours for a lengthy period of time. Ultimately, children need to build up to attending the full session as quickly as possible. Only when attending the whole session are children able to benefit fully from what the setting has to offer, to establish and maintain friendships and learn and conform to routines and rules.

The role of parents in the first few days

When first starting in a setting, many children are understandably anxious for their parents to stay with them until they feel secure. In most cases, it is reasonable for settings to expect a parent to stay with their child on their first day in the setting for as long as the child wishes. Parents should be made to feel welcome in the setting, and invited to take part in activities. After the first day, a setting may wish to encourage parents to try leaving their child for a while, to see how the child manages without them. If possible, parents should remain close by so that they can be called back if their child becomes upset and cannot be comforted. However, practitioners should be sensitive to parents' individual circumstances. Working parents may not have a great deal of flexibility, and may not be able to stay beyond the first day. If this is the case, parents should not be made to feel guilty about having to leave, and practitioners should aim to reassure them that everything will be fine.

For children who are still unwilling to be left by their parents after having had a reasonable length of time to settle into the setting, practitioners will need to discuss steps forward with parents. It can be very upsetting for all involved to see a distressed child, but thankfully most children are able to be distracted and consoled within a short period of time. Eventually, all children need to learn that their parents cannot stay with them for ever. This may mean a few difficult days, and staff should have at hand strategies to minimise the child's distress. Such strategies might include:

◆ encouraging the parents to let the child bring a comforter from home
◆ telling a child when his parent will be back, showing him where the hands need to move to on the clock
◆ distracting the child with a favourite activity.

Of course, if parents wish to stay in the setting as a volunteer to support children's learning this should be encouraged. However, it is still a good idea for their children to learn to separate from them, as they may not always be able to be in the setting.

Preparing the room

There are a number of things that practitioners may wish to do in order to be fully prepared and to have 'set the scene for positive behaviour' before a new group of children starts in the setting. These include:

◆ Preparing labels with photographs for children's coat pegs, trays, etc. These help the children to immediately feel secure and at home, and means that they are able to hang their own coats and know where to put their things right from the start.

♦ Making sure that the setting is clean and tidy and that all resources are in good repair. If children come into a messy setting with torn posters and books and broken toys, they are not being set a good example with regard to caring for things.

♦ Making sure that all things that practitioners wish the children to have access to are within their reach and clearly labelled. If there are things that children are not allowed to have unsupervised, they should be kept out of temptation's way, at least until the children have learnt the rules.

♦ Using the information gathered about likes and dislikes to ensure that some familiar and favourite activities and experiences are provided during children's first few days.

Chapter 2

Encouraging positive behaviour throughout the day

Timetabling the curriculum

A key principle for early years education is that in order to be effective, an early years curriculum should be carefully structured:

> There should be opportunities for children to engage in activities planned by adults and also those that they plan or initiate themselves. Well-planned purposeful activity and appropriate intervention by practitioners will engage children in the learning process.
>
> (Curriculum guidance for the foundation stage, QCA, 2000, p. 11)

It is crucial to get this balance right between adult-planned and child-planned or -initiated activities in order provide an environment in which children are most likely to behave positively. The curriculum guidance is also clear that well-planned play, both indoors and outdoors, is a key way in which young children learn with enjoyment and challenge.

Therefore, the curriculum and timetable that practitioners provide should be based upon high quality, well-planned play experiences, with opportunities for the children to develop their own interests and respond to their environment. Children do not distinguish between play and work, and neither should the practitioner. A timetable that consists of 'work' sessions followed by free play sessions is not appropriate for an early years setting, and is likely to lead to confrontations between children and practitioners, where the practitioner expects children to finish their 'work' before being allowed to play. The message given to the child is that the 'work' is the most important thing and that the 'play' is a treat that is earned by completing the work. Is this really an appropriate message to give young children?

Likely reasons for unwanted behaviour related to timetabling . . .	*and the solution*
The child becomes bored or frustrated at having to wait too long – waiting for the register to be taken; waiting for a drink; waiting for a turn at an activity; waiting to listen to a story; waiting to line up to wash hands.	While it is important for young children to learn that that they sometimes need to wait for things and to begin to develop patience, periods of waiting should be kept to a minimum in early years settings. Practitioners should try to make the most of every moment – time is too precious to be spent waiting and doing nothing for long periods of time.
The child does not want to do what the practitioner is asking him to. This should be seen as a message to the practitioner that the child is not interested in what has been planned. Children do not become effective learners by being coerced into activities that they do not like.	Practitioners should listen to the message and not insist on the child doing the activity unless absolutely necessary (hardly ever). They should ask: 'It is really important that he does this?' Most times, the answer will be 'no'.
The child has spent all day indoors.	Practitioners should provide free-flow play between the indoor and outdoor areas. Wet weather should not prevent children from going outside. Wellingtons and raincoats should be provided to allow children to splash in the puddles.
The child is tired.	Practitioners should plan to carry out activities that require high levels of concentration early in the day while the children are still fresh. A rest area should be provided where children can have a nap if they need to.
The child is not sure what is expected of her or does not know how to carry out an activity.	Practitioners should ensure that all activities that require it are explained fully, and that adults are at hand to give children appropriate support as needed.
The child has not had a turn at an activity he wishes to do.	Practitioners should aim to plan the timetable so that all children can have a turn at an activity at some point during the day. Where this is not possible (e.g. cooking), adults should spend time explaining to the children that they will have a turn in the future.

Likely reasons for unwanted behaviour related to timetabling . . .	*and the solution*
	However, with careful planning, it should nearly always be possible to involve every child (e.g. having a turn to stir the cake mixture).
The child has lost interest in an activity.	Practitioners should not always insist that children finish every activity. They should allow children to return to an activity at a later stage if and when they regain interest.
The child is frustrated at being asked to stop an activity she is enjoying.	Practitioners should plan for children to be able to carry out activities over extended periods of time. Children should be given warning *before* it is time to end the activity: 'In ten minutes we need to tidy up.' Practitioners should consider if they *really* need to tidy up. Could something be pushed to one side instead and returned to after lunch?
The child is expected to carry out a particular activity sitting at a table. Many young children find extended periods of sitting at a table difficult – it may be uncomfortable for them; they may feel restricted, or simply feel the urge to keep moving around.	Practitioners should be flexible about where they allow children to carry out activities. Unless for safety reasons, there are few activities that need to be completed at a table. Practitioners should remember that nearly all activities can be carried out outdoors as well as indoors.

Beginnings and endings

The start and end of the day, as well as beginnings and endings of individual activities, need careful consideration to maximise positive behaviour.

Upon arrival in the setting, it is strongly recommended that children are immediately able to begin an activity. There is no reason why children should be gathered in one spot in order to wait for a register to be taken. They will quickly become bored, and, as a result, they are less likely to behave as wanted. Instead, one adult can be responsible for greeting children and their parents and marking children's names in the register. Each child should be greeted by name with a smile. This helps to make both the practitioner and the child feel positive about the day to come. The children can then choose an activity and the other adults can immediately begin observing and interacting with children as they engage in their chosen activities.

Parents should feel welcome to come into the setting and should not be made to feel that they need to leave as soon as possible. If a child arrives upset, the practitioner should take the time to talk with the parent about the reason for this, and to acknowledge the child's feelings. Children may bring things to show the practitioner or other children, but it is best if these go home with Mum or Dad once they have been shown. If children make a fuss about parting with the toy, it is probably a good idea for practitioners to have a quiet word with parents and suggest that it may be best not to bring things to show from home. Allowing children to have toys from home in the setting is often a bad idea, as children tend to be particularly possessive over such toys, and squabbles are likely to result from other children trying to have a turn with the toy. Such toys may also become lost or broken, which is simply one more thing for the practitioner and child to worry about.

Children should be given adequate warning that activities will be coming to an end. A sand timer is a useful way of giving children this warning and enables children to see the passing of time and the approach of tidy-up time or another transition. If children are given no warning before they are asked to stop what they are doing, it is hardly surprising if some protest. As adults, most of us would be extremely annoyed if somebody turned off the television in the middle of our favourite programme, without warning. If possible, practitioners should tell children that they will be able to return to their activity later. If the children are constructing something, staff should consider whether it really has to be broken up and tidied away, or whether the half-finished construction can be stored in one piece so that the children can return to it. It can be very disheartening for children to have their creations dismantled on a daily basis, and may inadvertently give the message that they are not valued or important.

At the end of the day, it is a good idea for children to be told about some of the things that are planned for the next day. This prepares them for the day to come, and is a particularly useful strategy for children who benefit from being given warning of new things. If parents are ever late to pick up their children, practitioners should keep the children occupied rather than allowing them to become anxious or attention seeking. An adult could share a book or sing action songs with these children until their parents arrive. Children should be reassured that their parents will be there to collect them soon.

Drink, snack and mealtimes

Drink, snack and mealtimes often present particular difficulties for children whose behaviour has been raised as a concern. Much of this has to do with the fact that there is often a great deal of waiting associated with food and drink. In particular, children are often expected to wait for a considerable length of time after their lunch until all the other children have finished. While some practitioners use this time as an opportunity to engage in conversation with the children, in some settings children are simply expected to wait in silence. It is hardly surprising if these children begin to misbehave; their behaviour tells us that they are bored. Practitioners should ask themselves if it is really necessary for the children to sit unoccupied at the lunch table waiting for their peers to finish eating. In many settings, staffing is reduced during lunchtimes while staff take their own lunch break. For this reason, it may not be possible to give children free rein throughout the setting when they have finished eating. However, there should be no reason why children cannot go to a particular area – the book corner, for example – once they have finished eating. This arrangement would only need two members of staff

– one to supervise the children still eating and the other to supervise the children in the specified area.

It goes without saying that practitioners should *never* insist that children eat a particular food or finish what is on their plate. If a child is unwilling to eat something, it is either because he is full; does not like the food; *thinks* he does not like the food; or is feeling unwell. Children do not refuse food simply to challenge practitioners. If the adult tries to insist that the child eats the food, the child may begin to develop unpleasant associations around food, potentially leading to eating disorders in later life. At best, a confrontation is likely to develop between child and practitioner. Instead, practitioners should allow children to leave food, and at the end of the day let parents know if their child has eaten little or nothing.

Drink and snack times are a common feature in early years settings, but unfortunately tend to involve a great deal of waiting. If staff in a setting do decide that they wish to have a set drink or snack time, they should aim to make the most of it by getting children to prepare and serve the drinks and snacks. The other children should only be gathered together when the drinks are ready to be served, and adults should use the time to engage in conversation or discussion with the children. As with lunch, as soon as children have finished eating or drinking, they should be allowed to return to their activity.

If practitioners wish to create an environment that really does maximise opportunities for positive behaviour, a better option might be to implement a 'snack bar' system (see case study overleaf) whereby children choose if and when they wish to have a drink or snack.

Free-play sessions

As mentioned above, children benefit from extended periods of self-directed activity without unnecessary interruptions. Practitioners should have high expectations of children's behaviour during free play, and these should be communicated to the children. For example, it is desirable for children to be able to get out a resource that they wish to play with. However, if they do so, there should be an expectation that they will put the resource away again when they have finished playing with it, preferably without having to be told to do so by an adult. If this is new to the children, practitioners may find that the resources are sometimes left on the floor or table to begin with. However, most children soon rise to the responsibility given to them, and will learn to tidy away after themselves.

In any setting, one of the rules will relate to the sharing of resources, and adults should remind the children of this rule on a regular basis. Children should be taught to ask for a turn with a particular toy, and know how to respond if the child they are asking refuses. Practitioners need to keep a discrete eye on the group and sensitively intervene in any confrontations before they escalate.

If children are becoming over-excited during a free-play session and things risk getting out of hand, rather than reprimanding the children and stopping the play, a skilled practitioner may be able to join in with the play and subtly redirect it to calm things down. For example, if the children are pretending to be dinosaurs and chasing each other around the room trying to eat each other up, the practitioner could join the play as a dinosaur wizard with a magic wand. When she waves her magic wand at a dinosaur, it immediately falls asleep. If done well (e.g. with the practitioner using a funny voice and exaggerated body movements) the children

Case study: The snack bar at Mayflower Playgroup

Ever since Mayflower Playgroup had been set up, there had always been a snacktime during which all the children were gathered together in a circle for a drink and biscuit. All the children were expected to take part, but it was sometimes difficult to persuade children who were in the middle of an activity. Once gathered in the circle, there tended to be quite a lot of bickering between the children, and the practitioners always felt that it was too noisy.

At the suggestion of an educational psychologist, the playgroup decided to end the formal snack time and set up a snack bar instead. This consisted of a table with four chairs. On the table there was always a tray of cups, a jug of water, and a jug of milk or juice. There was also a bowl of cut fruit on the table each day.

When children were hungry or thirsty, they could go to the snack bar without needing to ask an adult. Children were expected to wash their hands first, which they quickly learnt to do. The rule was that children had to sit down to have a drink or snack, which meant that a maximum of four children could be at the snack bar at any one time. The children poured their own drink, refilling the water jug from the tap as necessary. There was a poster showing how much fruit they should take (e.g. one half of orange; two pieces of apple). To begin with, some children took more fruit than they were supposed to, but this was noticed by other children, and soon stopped. If a child was unsure about how much fruit to take, there were always other children on hand to help with the counting. When children had finished eating and drinking, they washed their cup and returned it to the tray.

The snack bar has proved to be a great success. The children enjoy the responsibility involved and are pleased at being able to engage in activities for an extended period of time without being expected to stop for snack time. Other than an occasional spilt jug, the snack bar has always run smoothly.

are likely to accept the change to the game without question. The practitioner could then initiate a dinosaur snoring competition, or have a contest to see which dinosaur could stay still the longest.

It is very common for children to engage in superhero play during free-play sessions. Many practitioners are very quick to intervene in superhero scenarios, particularly where pretend weapons are involved, reminding the children that 'guns aren't allowed in this nursery'. Such concerns are understandable, but some children risk having their play constantly interrupted by adults. There appears to be no clear consensus among experts about whether pretend weapon play is good or bad for children. However, research suggests that children who participate in superhero play become skilled in their movements, distinguish between real and feigned aggression, and learn to regulate each other's activity. Such play can also help children learn how to face their own fears and is also a good outlet for them to act out, which all children need to do on a regular basis.

While practitioners may wish to ban all pretend weapons, it could be argued that this is unrealistic. Children will make pretend weapons from Lego or newspaper, or simply make their fingers into the shape of a gun. They quickly learn to conceal their pretend weapons from practitioners, only to brandish them again as soon as the adult's back is turned. Rather than engaging in a constant no-win battle of wills with children over pretend weapons, practitioners can use children's interest in violent pretend play as an opportunity to discuss right and wrong and to teach them about the dangers of real weapons.

Instead of banning superhero play, practitioners should set clear but realistic boundaries and enforce these consistently. Such boundaries might include rules that superhero play can only take place outside and that the children must not actually touch each other. If superhero play does ever get out of hand, practitioners should use this opportunity to explain why violence and aggression is not acceptable, and to make sure that the child understands that superheroes exist in order to help other people.

Structured sessions

The importance of free play has been highlighted. However, more structured activities are also very valuable. Indeed, some children respond particularly well to structure, and feel more confident if their activities are highly structured. As a general rule, more structured sessions should be optional. As stated earlier, children learn little from things that do not interest them, and can easily feel anxious, frustrated or resentful if they are asked to do activities against their wishes.

Structured sessions should generally be closely supervised by an adult, as the potential for failure is much greater than with self-directed activities. However, children should be allowed to have a go at things for themselves without an adult taking over at the first sign of difficulty. Practitioners should avoid over-emphasis on a finished product that is expected to look a particular way. If children feel that their completed Mother's Day card has to look exactly like the practitioner's, they are likely to be disappointed. Repeated disappointments of this kind can have a negative effect upon children's motivation and self-esteem, and may lead to inappropriate behaviour. In creative activities, the emphasis should always be upon the process rather than the product. If children ask for help, they should be given just enough to help them complete the task, without the adult taking over.

Structured activities should ideally be quite short, as many young children find it difficult to sustain concentration. Adults should plan in such a way that enables children to begin a structured activity and then return to it later in the day or week.

Dealing with unexpected events

Young children benefit from a predictable environment in which, for most of the time, they know what is going to happen next. They quickly become familiar with schedules and routines and feel secure in the knowledge that they know what to do in given situations. Practitioners should aim to provide a predictable and consistent environment to enhance this feeling of security. Of course, no environment can ever be completely predictable, and children also need to learn to deal with new and unexpected events. For some children, this can be particularly difficult or distressing, and unwanted behaviours may develop as a result.

Practitioners should aim to prepare children for new situations and events wherever possible. Many can be predicted, even if the exact timing is not known. For example, in a nursery school it is likely that a fire drill will take place at some point. In preparation for this event, the practitioner could read the children a story about a fire engine and then explain that sometimes there are fire drills in nurseries. The practitioner should explain why fire drills take place and tell the children what to expect. Wherever possible, when a new or unexpected event takes place, the children should be told exactly what is happening, rather than simply being given a series of orders to follow. Of course, in an emergency, there may not be time to do this, which makes it all the more important to rehearse unexpected events in advance of them occurring.

Practitioners may wish to make books about things that might happen in order to help prepare children for these new or unexpected events. For example, a book could be made about a dentist's visit to the setting. If photos are taken when the dentist visits, a book can be made to be used with future groups of children. The book can then be read to the children before the event next takes place. Parents of children who find new or unexpected events particularly difficult could borrow the book to share at home with their child on the evening before the new event. When an event is known about in advance, settings should plan to have additional adult support available to those children who are known to find new things difficult.

Using a visual timetable

Visual timetables provide a useful way of helping children to understand the routine of the setting day and to know what is going to happen next. They have traditionally been used with children on the autistic spectrum or those with delayed language skills, but are increasingly being used with whole groups of children as practitioners become aware of their benefits.

In its simplest form, a visual timetable can simply be a strip of card along which visual representations of the activities and events of the day are arranged in chronological order. The timetable may be arranged horizontally or vertically. Children can look along or down the timetable to see the order of events. For example:

free-play→carpet-time→swimming→lunch→adult-led activity→story→home

Commercially made visual timetables are available, with sets of activity cards. However, a home-made timetable can be made quite simply by practitioners. Taking photographs of objects and activities in the setting is a particularly good idea, as these will be more recognisable and meaningful to children than the cartoon drawings in the commercially produced activity cards. The timetable itself can be made from a strip of thick card (perhaps laminated for extra durability). The activity cards can be attached with Velcro or Blu-tack.

To begin with, practitioners will need to explain the timetable to children. When an activity has been completed, the corresponding card can be removed from the timetable. Some timetables have a 'finished' box at the bottom into which children can put the card. Most children particularly enjoy being chosen to remove cards from the timetable and put them into the finished box. This activity can help the child to understand beginnings, endings and sequences.

Catching the child being good: the importance of praise

Throughout the day, practitioners should be constantly looking for opportunities to praise children. This strategy is often referred to as 'catching the child being good'. A useful exercise is for practitioners to practice going around the setting praising each child at least once. The praise should be justified rather than contrived, as children can be very good at knowing when adults are being insincere. Many of us are much more used to focusing upon behaviours that trouble us and tend to forget how much of the time the majority of children are behaving as we would wish them to. Praise given should be *specific*, in the form of statements such as 'I really like the way you're sitting/helping/sharing' etc. Once practitioners become used to 'catching the child being good' it becomes second nature. When a particular child has behaved in a particularly worrying way, the practitioner should set herself a target of 'catching him being good' at least ten times that day. This can help to put things into perspective and remind the practitioner that even the most challenging child behaves appropriately far more often than inappropriately. Behaviour that is rewarded is more likely to be repeated, and this applies both to negative as well as positive behaviours. For this reason, low-level inappropriate behaviour should be ignored wherever possible, and the practitioner should instead aim to identify behaviours that can be praised.

Almost without exception, children enjoy being praised. For a very small number of children who have perhaps not received much praise in the past, it can take them a while to get used to being praised. To begin with, they may be embarrassed by a practitioner's praise and not know quite how to respond to it. Over time, the child will get used to praise and learn to respond positively. Practitioners should be aware that some shy or withdrawn children may prefer 'private' praise instead of being praised in front of the whole group.

Chapter 3

Structuring the learning environment to encourage positive behaviour

A great deal of unwanted behaviour can be a direct result of the way in which the learning environment is structured within a setting. In order to see more of the behaviour that is wanted, therefore, it makes sense to look carefully at the learning environment and see what changes might be made to support children's behaviour. These changes include changes to the layout and physical aspects of the setting as well as changes to resources and the way in which they are used.

Layout of the room

Early years settings vary enormously in their size, shape and layout. Although little can be done to change size and shape of the building itself, the way in which the rooms are laid out and resourced can easily be changed, and such changes may bring about positive changes in children's behaviour.

Some small settings make the mistake of having too many tables, meaning that there is little remaining space for non table-based activities that should make up the bulk of children's learning in the early years. It is hard to think of an occasion on which all children in a setting would need to be seated at a table simultaneously. Whole group table-based activities are not advisable, as such activities are likely to be imposed by adults rather than chosen by children. Expecting all children to sit at a table and carry out an activity at the same time is a recipe for disaster. It very likely that some of the children will not want to do the activity, leading to resentment, lack of interest or confrontation.

If staff do want all children to do a particular table-based activity, the best way is to do this is in 'shifts', with perhaps half a dozen children at a time. In this way, the children who are less keen can have an appropriate level of adult support to motivate, encourage and assist them.

Many settings manage well with only two or three tables, leaving much more space for children to play and explore freely. Generally speaking, children should be allowed to choose their own seats for table-based activities, unless there is a good reason not to. Separating young children because 'they're trouble together' sends a very negative message to children and is unlikely to improve behaviour in a meaningful way. The practitioner's time is better spent on thinking about the reasons for the clash between children and working on improving their relationship.

Practitioners should ensure that there is adequate space around tables for children to get past without knocking against those sitting down. A child who has his elbow jogged while putting the finishing touches to a drawing is likely to be frustrated or upset by this, and conflict may result. The same principle applies to the block play area and any other areas where children are working on a 'product' that is easily damaged or spoiled. Similarly, thought should be given as to the positioning of activities and areas in relation to each other. Placing the sand tray next to a cooking activity, for example, is not a good idea, for obvious reasons.

Areas that are likely to be especially popular, such as the home corner/imaginative play area should be as large as possible, to enable more children to play there. Some settings set a limit on the number of children that are allowed to play in such areas at any one time. However, the *way* in which the children are playing in the area is more important than the actual number. It would be better to have a more flexible policy whereby as many children as want to can play, provided that they do so sensibly, sharing resources and not arguing with others. If an area does become so overcrowded that it poses a safety risk, it is better for an adult to say 'Who would like to come and play with me?' rather than having to choose some unlucky children to leave the area against their will.

The 'thinking chair'

The 'thinking chair' can be a helpful strategy to encourage positive behaviour. The rationale behind using such a strategy is based upon two main assumptions:

◆ that all children have a need to feel liked and respected
◆ that all children have the right to be taught how to behave in such a way that they are liked and respected by other children (and adults).

There are times when, for a number of reasons, a child's behaviour becomes unacceptable. At such times, the child should be given the opportunity to stop and think about what she has done, and what she could have done to make things better both for her as well as for others.

Having an identified physical object, such as the thinking chair, cushion or beanbag provides:

◆ a safe opportunity to remove the child from the situation that is causing distress
◆ time and motivation for the child to think about what kind of behaviour will enable her to return to the group.

The practitioner uses the thinking chair in a positive way by openly acknowledging that we all make mistakes. When we are carrying strong feelings because something has upset us we may need space away to reflect and to repair what has gone wrong. It is very important that the chair is used in this positive way, not as a punishment. For this reason, it should never be referred to as the 'naughty chair' or another term that labels the child and potentially damages self-esteem. Similarly, although the chair should be positioned away from the centre of the group, it should not be positioned in an 'unpleasant' area, such as an untidy, dimly lit corner of the room.

The chair should be introduced to the whole group before being used, when the group is calm and contented, and practitioners should explain why it may be used and exactly how it will be used, if needed. It should be emphasised that the chair is there to help children, not to punish them. It may be useful at this stage for practitioners to tell children about a time when they themselves were angry or upset, and how they needed time on their own to calm down and think about the situation.

If the chair does need to be used, it can be very useful to have a pre-arranged script that is used by all adults consistently. The script is most effective if practitioners focus on themselves as the people who will assist the child in dealing with unwanted behaviours. For example, the practitioner says: 'I can't let you hit/bite/kick' rather than 'Stop hitting/biting/kicking'. In this way, the practitioner can reassure the child that it is the behaviour that is not liked, rather than the child herself. At the same time, the adult is clearly establishing boundaries by saying 'I can't let you'. This also reassures the child that the adult is in control.

The use of the thinking chair can be illustrated by *Case study: Claire.*

Managing tantrums

There may be times when children become extremely angry or upset, and at such times they may resist requests to go to the thinking chair. While it is acceptable for the adult to lead the child by the hand to the thinking chair, it is clearly not acceptable to pull a child who refuses this. If the child will not go to the thinking chair or a similar designated place, the adult should acknowledge their refusal, saying, for example, 'I'm sorry you don't want to go to the thinking chair. Perhaps we can talk about this later when you're feeling better'. Then the adult should move away from the child, avoiding confrontation. Other children should be

Case study: Claire

Claire is three and a half years old and has just started at her local nursery. She settles quickly and enjoys a range of activities in the group. However, when she can't have something she wants, or when another child takes something from her, she often hits, bites or kicks.

Staff think that Claire would benefit from the thinking chair. All the children in the group are introduced to the chair and told about how and why it might be used. In future, when Claire hits, bites or kicks, her keyworker or another adult intervenes by establishing eye contact with Claire and saying firmly but in a quiet voice: 'No Claire, I can't let you hit/bite/kick'. Claire is then led to the thinking chair for two or three minutes until staff can observe that she is ready to rejoin the group. Alongside this strategy, Claire is taught to ask other children for a turn with toys and to tell adults when another child has taken something from her.

asked to leave the area, so that the child does not receive any additional attention. If the child's behaviour is extremely disruptive, dangerous or upsetting to other children, practitioners may wish to consider removing the rest of the group to a different area of the setting, leaving only the child and a supervising adult. This may seem like a drastic measure, but it is far better than the child's peers congregating around to witness the child's loss of control. Other children may easily become agitated, confused or frightened by witnessing a severe tantrum. If the child's tantrum takes the form of screaming, shouting or stamping feet, with no damage to others or to property, it is usually best to ignore it. It is not generally productive at this time to try and reason with the child, as she will be overwhelmed by her feelings.

Although restraint of children has been referred to as 'therapeutic physical intervention' (Morgan, 2004), it is difficult to see restraint as a positive strategy. However, on very rare occasions it may be necessary. Clearly, restraint should only be used as a last resort to prevent injuries or serious damage to property. For example, if the child is throwing heavy objects at other children's heads, it might be necessary to restrain the child if the other children cannot be immediately removed from the area. It is very important that practitioners have training in how to restrain children correctly, holding them in a safe and comfortable position, as restraint can be dangerous if done incorrectly. If a child does need to be restrained, this should only be for as long as is necessary to prevent injury to the child or others, or severe damage to property.

Once the child has calmed down, the adult should address the incident (e.g. encouraging the child to apologise to another child she smacked) and then move on, resolving with the child to make a 'fresh start'. Once an incident has been dealt with, practitioners should avoid referring to it again.

Tantrums are not uncommon in young children, but if a child has regular tantrums in her setting, practitioners may wish to seek support from outside professionals to help them address her behaviour in a positive way.

The 'nurture corner'

Some early years settings have set up a 'nurture corner' to good effect. The idea is similar to that of the thinking chair, to provide a safe place where children can go if they are angry or upset. However, whereas children are usually prompted to go to the thinking chair when they have displayed unwanted behaviour, the nurture corner is an area that children can choose to go to whenever they wish. There is no one single way to organise a nurture corner; practitioners can use their imagination and creativity to decide how it will look and how it will work. The following ideas have all worked well:

◆ Beanbags, cushions and other soft seating are used to create a comfortable area.
◆ Screens or room dividers are used to create a well-defined, separate space that allows children some privacy.
◆ Posters and artwork depicting different emotions are used to decorate the area.
◆ Teddies and other soft toys are provided for cuddling.

- Paper and drawing media are provided so that children can draw a picture about how they are feeling.
- A box of tissues is provided for children who wish to have a cry.
- Adults keep a discreet eye on the nurture corner, and ask any children using it if they would like some company, or to talk.
- Alternatively, a reversible sign can be used for the children to display. One side reads 'I would like some time by myself' and the other side reads 'Please come and talk to me'.
- Rules are established with the children over the use of the nurture corner. These might include expected behaviour within the corner (e.g. no shouting) and a rule that the corner is not simply to be used to avoid doing something such as tidying up.

Encouraging positive behaviour outdoors

As stated in Chapter 2, children in early years settings should wherever possible have free-flow play between the indoor and outdoor parts of the setting. A great deal of unwanted behaviour results from children being kept indoors unnecessarily. All activities that can be carried out indoors can also take place outside, often with minimal adaptation. The outdoor area provides space that allows for free and rapid movement between different areas, something that is not usually possible indoors. When thinking about rules, practitioners should take account of the fact that what might be considered to be inappropriate behaviour indoors is perfectly appropriate for the outdoor area. Shouting and running are two examples of such behaviour. Both come naturally to young children, and while they are generally discouraged indoors (for good reason), it would be inappropriate to forbid such behaviour outside. This would be likely to lead to stress, resentment and confrontation.

When planning and arranging the outdoor environment, careful thought should to be given to the use and placement of resources. Many disputes and confrontations outdoors revolve around bicycles and similar wheeled toys. For many practitioners, arguments over 'whose turn it is on the bike' are the most common outdoor tensions. No matter how many other enticing activities are provided, bicycles are always a favourite, and it makes sense for there to be a reasonable number of them so that children do not have to wait all week for a turn. However, too many bikes in an area can dominate the space and be intimidating for some children, restricting quality of play. Nevertheless, where there are fewer bikes than children wanting to ride them, there will always be the potential for conflict, and practitioners need to come up with a method of ensuring fair and trouble-free turn taking.

In recognition of the fact that boys tend to dominate bike riding in settings, some settings have single-sex bike riding sessions to ensure that girls have fair access to bicycles. This may work well to begin with, when boys often succeed in getting girls off the bikes just by looking at them. Ultimately though, it is better if practitioners are able to devise a system that allows both boys and girls fair access to bikes (or any other resource) in a mixed-sex group. The following case study demonstrates how this was done in one nursery school.

Case study: Nursery bike-hire

In a large nursery school, practitioners were unhappy at having to deal with frequent arguments over bikes. Following a staff meeting to discuss possible solutions, a bike-hire scheme was set up, whereby an adult acted as an attendant at the 'bike-hire stand' (made from milk crates) in the outdoor play area. Children are able to 'hire' bikes for slots of up to fifteen minutes and are given a permit that is attached to the handlebars to show that they are the rightful rider. As this nursery has free-flow play all day, each child is guaranteed at least one bike hire per day. The adult has a hire book to keep track of the hiring and ensure that all children who want to ride a bike are given equal access. Children who have already hired a bike earlier in the day can only hire again if all other children who wish to have had a turn. With some training and supervision, children are now being taught take on the role of bike-hire attendant. Some children even prefer this to riding the bikes! The children have designed a uniform for the bike-hire attendant and a parent has kindly made this up for them using her sewing machine.

Playing outside should be treated as a right, not a privilege, and for this reason it is not appropriate to stop children from accessing the outdoor area as a sanction for inappropriate behaviour. However, as an extra incentive to good behaviour, children can be rewarded by being given an opportunity to do a favourite outdoor activity that is not regularly available.

Using ICT to support children's behaviour

In a research report published by the DfES (Passey et al., 2004), many teachers reported that children are better behaved in lessons when ICT is used, and this was supported by pupil reports. Some teachers and other professionals believed that from an early age ICT may help to support higher literacy levels, and this could lead to reduced truancy, crime and anti-social behaviour over time.

Computers and other information and communication technologies such as digital cameras are now increasingly found in early years settings. Even very young children are proving to be remarkably adept at mastering computer skills, and using a computer is generally a favourite activity in settings. Some practitioners may feel that young children should be engaging in more 'practical' and physical hands-on activities in preference to using a computer, but there is no research evidence to suggest that computers in early years settings have a detrimental effect upon young children's development. On the contrary, for some children, including those with disabilities and additional needs, ICT allows them to develop their skills and access activities that they may otherwise be unable to do. For less confident children and those with learning difficulties, carefully chosen computer programs can enable them to build their confidence and achieve success, increasing motivation and self-esteem in the process. Practitioners can monitor the use of the computer(s) to ensure that children access an appropriate balance of activities throughout the day.

As with bikes, arguments can sometimes arise over whose turn it is to use the computer. Practitioners will need to think of a fair way in which children can access the computer, and this needs to be explained to them so that they understand the system. Some settings use sand timers to give children a visual prompt as to when their time is up. However, this is not necessarily the best system if children are playing a computer game, as it is understandably very frustrating to be told that one's time is up midway through a game. In such instances, the rule should perhaps be one or two games per child, rather than a rigid period of time. Children can be encouraged to work at a computer in pairs, but adults may need to supervise this quite closely to begin with to ensure that both children have equal access and that arguments do not arise.

As a preferred activity, a turn on the computer can be a useful incentive where practitioners are using a reward scheme to support children's behaviour. For children who would benefit from having a personalised reward scheme, adults who feel reasonably confident in using a computer can create professional-looking reward charts using basic software. A word processing program together with clipart can be used to make charts that focus on the child's interests, such as trains, dolls or animals.

Settings that do not have a computer may wish to consider fundraising to buy one. Alternatively, many large companies regularly upgrade their computer systems and can sometimes be persuaded to donate their old computers to education settings.

Animals in the setting

Having animals in the setting – either on a permanent basis or as visitors – can provide a powerful opportunity for children to learn self-control, empathy, perspective-taking and caring skills. A wealth of research evidence demonstrates the therapeutic effect of animals. Charities such as Pets as Therapy take dogs and cats into hospitals, hospices, residential homes and day care centres in order to enhance the happiness and well-being of residents and patients. Animals can be used in a similar way to support positive behaviour in children. Animals such as guinea pigs and rabbits, if fully tame, can be petted and stroked (under the supervision of an adult) and can be enormously comforting to upset children. Smaller rodents and insects might not have the same 'cuddly' properties, but children will still benefit from being taught how to care for them and meet their needs. Some settings with large outdoor areas keep chickens, and the children benefit enormously from rearing the chicks, caring for the adult birds and collecting their eggs. Outdoor areas will often contain animals in their natural habitats, such as worms, snails and ants. Clearly, caring for animals requires children to be very responsible. Many children whose behaviour challenges us respond very well to this type of responsibility, showing marked improvements in both their behaviour and self-esteem.

The decision to keep animals in the setting should not be taken lightly. The welfare of the animals is paramount, and they must not be allowed to become stressed, frightened or aggressive due to over-handling or inappropriate handling. Nocturnal animals are not recommended, for obvious reasons. Practitioners should ensure appropriate spaces and conditions for animals, and must consider arrangements for caring for animals over weekends and during holidays.

If your setting does not feel that it is possible or desirable to keep animals (e.g. if a child or member of staff is allergic to fur) animal visits can still be arranged. A setting might arrange for parents to bring their pet to the group to show the children, and to talk about its care. Alternatively, many charities such as Pets as Therapy and the Guide Dogs for the Blind Association are happy to visit schools with their animals and talk about their work.

Music in the setting

There is a body of evidence that demonstrates the positive impact music has upon children's learning. Childhood songs, rhymes, movement and musical games are important as they provide children with opportunities to develop a range of skills vital to language acquisition. They may also help young children to develop inner speech and impulse control and this can contribute to the development of self-management of behaviour.

When stressed, blood pressure rises and the heart races. Evidence suggests that if this happens too often, it can increase the risk of cardiovascular disease. Chafin et al. (2004) found that listening to soothing classical music can reduce levels of stress (and thus lower blood pressure) much more quickly than listening to pop or jazz music or being in a music-free environment. Although this research was carried out with adults, is seems reasonable to suggest that classical music might be a good way of helping an angry or upset child to recover.

There are many different ways in which a nursery setting can use music to enhance positive behaviours. These include the following.

Incorporating music into the daily routine

Daily routines such as greetings and goodbyes, picking up toys, tidying up, washing hands and mealtimes can be taught and reinforced through songs. This can make a less popular activity such as tidying up much more fun, with less chance of unwanted behaviour. In some early years settings, the popular children's action song 'This is the way we (e.g. tidy up; put away blocks; sweep the floor)' has been used to make tidying up into one of the children's favourite activities.

Teaching listening skills

Children who have difficulty listening often also have language difficulties and may later experience problems in other areas of the curriculum. Early years settings are ideal places to teach children to listen to a wide variety of music. Classical music can affect a child's behaviour in different ways. For example, pieces by Bach, Mozart and Chopin might have a therapeutic effect, while pieces by Wagner can have an energising effect. Practitioners can experiment with music by different composers, noting the effect this has on the children, and using this knowledge to their advantage. For example, when the children have become over-excited, a calming piece of music can be used to diffuse the excitement. In one setting, the turning-on of a CD player playing classical music is a signal to the children to stop what they are doing and listen. This provides a good way of getting the children's attention and immediately quieting a noisy room. It also saves practitioners having to ask the children to be quiet.

It is important to be aware that having music playing all the time can detract from a child learning to listen. Children and adults quickly learn to shut out sound if it is constant, as we know from our own experiences of being in noisy environments such as airports. For this reason, it is not recommended that background music is played throughout the day in settings. Instead, the children can be encouraged to listen to music at certain points during the day. Classical music tapes can also be used in a listening corner, where children may choose to sit and wear headphones to listen to music.

Active music making

Children can be given opportunities to take part in singing, dancing/movement and playing instruments (including those they have made themselves). They should have the opportunity to experiment with uncomplicated instruments such as drums, rhythm sticks and rattles on a regular basis.

Rules for the setting

It is very important that all practitioners have a shared understanding of the behaviour they are seeking to encourage in children. Similarly, there must be a clear consensus as to which behaviours are deemed to be unacceptable. There is no definitive list of what constitutes 'unacceptable behaviour' – this will depend on the context and individual setting. The task of practitioners is to decide what is *unacceptable for their setting*.

A useful starting point might be to hold a staff meeting to discuss practitioners' perceptions and understanding of the term 'unacceptable behaviour'. Following this discussion, the following definition may be used to help decide which behaviours to target when thinking about rule making:

> Unacceptable behaviour can be defined as any behaviour that has a negative effect upon the achievement or happiness of others or oneself.

Of course, this is not the only way to define unacceptable behaviour, but this particular definition can help staff to put things into perspective and to think about the things that really matter when deciding the setting's rules. For example, is it really necessary to have a rule which states that children must cross their legs when sitting on the carpet? Not all children find sitting cross-legged comfortable, making it difficult for them to comply. If a setting has a large enough seating area then it should be possible for the children to sit with their legs in front of them without making unwanted contact with other children. A more appropriate rule might be: *We keep our arms and legs to ourselves.*

Staff should be able to justify every rule that is put in place in the setting. Having a rule simply because 'That's always been the rule' or because 'Other nurseries/playgroups have this rule' is not enough. If staff are not able to justify the rules to which they expect children to conform, how can children be expected to understand the importance of the rule and to comply with it?

Practitioners must remember that the rules they have set may not be the same as those in place in the child's home. This is another reason why staff should emphasise that certain behaviours are *unacceptable for the setting*. For example, practitioners are likely to decide that swearing is unacceptable behaviour in their setting and have a rule to this effect. If and when a child swears, the response should be along the lines of 'We don't swear in our nursery' rather than 'Swearing is very bad'. A number of children will be exposed to swearing at home, and the latter response gives the child the message that their parents are doing something bad. Of course, you may well disapprove of parents swearing in front of their children, but you must accept that you have no control over what happens in the child's home. It is unfair to the child to give the message that their parents' behaviour is unacceptable. If you ever do need to challenge parents' behaviour (for example, if a parent swears at their child in your setting), this should be done sensitively and out of earshot of the child. Only in exceptional and unavoidable circumstances should you challenge a parent in front of their child. Such exchanges are likely to be confusing, distressing and humiliating for the child.

Once rules have been decided, a consistent approach between *all* adults in the setting is vital. If one member of staff allows a child to poke his tongue out, tousling his hair and saying affectionately, 'You cheeky boy!' while another reprimands the child for the same gesture, the child will initially be confused – Is it all right to poke out my tongue or not? Of course, many children quickly learn that they can get away with certain things with certain adults, and adjust their behaviour accordingly depending on whose company they are in. Others remain confused about whether the behaviour is acceptable or not, and may continue to receive smiles from some adults and reprimands from others for the same behaviour. Children deserve a consistent approach in their early years setting, with clear boundaries that are applied in the same way by all adults. Practitioners can only expect positive behaviour if they provide clear and consistent rules and boundaries at all times.

Guidelines for setting and using rules

◆ Involve the children in rule making: ask for their ideas and suggestions.
◆ Phrase rules using positive language, in terms of what the children *are* to do, rather than what they are *not* to do. For example: *We listen when other people are talking* rather than: *We don't interrupt*.
◆ Aim for a maximum of six rules which are wide in their coverage. For example, a rule such as *We are kind to each other* can replace: *We don't fight*; *We don't call each other unkind names*; *We don't damage other people's property*; *We don't snatch toys from each other* and so on. If there are too many rules, it will be difficult for children to remember them.
◆ To decide whether each rule is appropriate, practitioners should ask themselves, 'Is this rule about a behaviour that has a negative effect upon children's achievement or happiness?'
◆ Discuss the rules with the children on a daily basis.
◆ Display the rules in a prominent place in the setting. Illustrate each rule with photographs of children following it.
◆ Invite children to draw and paint pictures of themselves following the rules and make a book using these pictures.
◆ Praise children every time they follow the rules: 'Well done Karim! You're being very kind to Josh.'

◆ When a child breaks a rule, state the rule calmly but firmly and give the child a chance to change their behaviour.
◆ Try not to give too much attention to the child who has broken the rule. Instead, praise other children who are following the rule.
◆ Have high expectations of children's behaviour, but when rules are broken, deal with the issue and then move on. Reassure children that no one is perfect, and encourage them to try hard to follow the rule in future.
◆ It is important that children feel confident to tell an adult when someone has hurt or upset them. Through discussion, help them to understand the difference between this and 'telling tales' to get other children into trouble for minor infractions of rules.

Using and allocating adults to maximise positive behaviour

As human beings, the overwhelming majority of us seek attention from others. Children are no different; in fact, children probably crave attention more than adults, as their own internal resources and patience are less well developed. In early years settings, it makes sense to use adults in such a way that children receive as much attention and support as possible, with the majority of attention being given to desired behaviours. If children are given plenty of attention when they are behaving as wanted, unwanted behaviours are less likely to occur.

On a day when the group is calm, on-task and apparently self-sufficient, it may be tempting for one or more of the practitioners in a setting to catch up on some paperwork, or put up a display. However, this temptation should be resisted. Instead, practitioners should take the opportunity to give some additional attention to a child or children they feel would benefit from it. Such attention need not necessarily involve direct contact – all children need space at times to develop their own play and ideas and to engage in problem-solving without adult intervention. If the practitioner judges it best not to directly intervene with the child's activity, a perfect opportunity exists for observation. It is often difficult to find the time to carry out prolonged observation, and practitioners should make the most of such opportunities. Practitioners could focus their observation upon a child who sometimes displays unwanted behaviours. What is different about today that has led to the child being calm, focused and behaving appropriately? Observation will be discussed in more detail in Chapter 6.

Practitioners should structure the day in such a way that there are never any occasions on which some adults are unused. This is a waste of the setting's most valuable resource – its staff. If you have a whole-group story-time, what do the rest of the adults do while one is reading to the children? Instead of 'spare' adults 'policing' the group and dealing with any children who are not listening or otherwise disrupting the story, it may be a better idea to split the children into smaller groups for story-time, each one led by a different adult in a separate area. In these smaller groups, there will be less scope for unwanted behaviours and more opportunities to engage individual children in the story, to ask them questions and to check their understanding of the text.

The most common reason for children behaving inappropriately during story-time is that they are finding it difficult to concentrate on the story, usually because they cannot understand the text. Clearly, practitioners should ensure that books chosen are accessible, interesting and large enough to be seen by all children in the group. A 'spare' adult could support a story with story props while another reads in order to allow children with delayed language skills or those at the early stages of acquiring English as an additional language to understand the text.

If a particular child or group of children is having difficulty behaving as wanted, the setting may decide to allocate additional adult support to that child or group. Engaging the child in a group activity is usually preferable to one-to-one support, but practitioners will obviously use their professional judgement. A child who is finding it particularly difficult to behave as wanted may appreciate and benefit from some one-to-one adult attention. Where this is the case, the adult should aim to give the child attention for positive behaviours, giving frequent praise. Where the child is engaging in unwanted behaviour, attention should be withdrawn unless the child is doing something that puts him or others at risk of harm. Of course, very few settings have the luxury of an over-generous adult–child ratio, but practitioners should still aim to identify times during the day when it is possible to give some extra support to those children who would benefit from it.

Chapter 4

Providing equality of opportunity and resisting stereotypes

Responding positively to individual needs, learning styles and interests

While certain sections of the press might have the public believe that nearly all children are potential 'thugs', just waiting for the opportunity to engage in violent or anti-social behaviour, some groups of children may be seen as particularly troublesome. Children from low socioeconomic groups, children of Travellers, African-Caribbean boys, children with learning difficulties and children from so-called 'problem families' are among those who risk being pre-judged before they have even stepped through the door of a setting. Siblings of children who have previously attended a setting and whose behaviour was of concern may automatically be assumed to have behaviour similar to that of their elder brother or sister.

The debate over which terms to use to describe children's behaviour continues. Practitioners who shun terms such as 'naughty', 'bad' and 'troublemaker' are sometimes accused of being overly politically correct. Their protagonists argue that children who 'misbehave' need to be told in no uncertain terms that they have been 'bad' and need to understand the error of their ways. While it is true that children do need to understand what are acceptable and unacceptable behaviours in their setting, and to comply with boundaries, the use of negative labels does not help children to adjust their behaviour. 'Naughty' labels are easily internalised by the child; if a child is told he is 'naughty', how can he behave otherwise? By definition, a naughty boy does naughty things. How is he expected to change if he has been labelled as naughty? Children tend to conform to the expectations others have of them. For this reason, it is vital that children are told that their *behaviour* is unacceptable (not them as individuals), and *why*. It may be obvious to us as adults why a particular behaviour is unacceptable, but to the child it may not be so obvious, especially if he has been allowed to engage in this behaviour at home or in another context.

Stereotyping

The term stereotyping refers to the creation of an oversimplified image of a particular group of people, usually by assuming that all members of the group are alike. Stereotypes inevitably affect what a person thinks and believes about others, as well as how s/he behaves towards them. Stereotypes are usually negative (e.g. 'black boys are disrespectful') but may also be nominally positive (e.g. 'Chinese children are very well-behaved'). However, even so-called positive stereotypes can be damaging. Using the given example, a young Chinese boy who is finding it difficult to conform to the standards of behaviour expected in his play-group may be seen by staff to be particularly troublesome, as Chinese children are 'supposed to be well-behaved.' Similarly, if the child's mother is aware of the stereotype, she may worry that there is something 'wrong' with her child as he is not conforming to the stereotype. It is easy to see how the child's mother could potentially end up feeling guilty or ashamed because her son is not behaving 'as Chinese boys should'.

To a certain extent, some degree of stereotyping is inevitable – as human beings we learn to make sense of the world through ordering and categorising objects and people. However, it is important that we are aware of the stereotypes we hold and how these may influence our interactions with others. While statistical analysis may demonstrate that a particular group of people is more or less likely to behave in a particular way, crude statistics tell us nothing about the individual. Nor do they tell us if a tendency towards a certain way of behaving is the result of some innate characteristic common to that group, or the result of the way in which that group is treated. Even if 99 per cent of a particular group was found to behave in a particular way (extremely unlikely), we should guard against assuming that a person we met from that group is part of the 99 per cent. Early years practitioners should never make assumptions about a child (or parent) and should always be aware that she might well belong to the 1 per cent that contradicts the stereotype. Each child should always be treated as a unique individual. Being a particular gender, race, age or class are all part of the child's identity, but the child's uniqueness cannot be defined solely in terms of the groups of which she is part.

Gender stereotyping and discrimination

Gender stereotyping is still very prevalent is modern society, and even very young children are constantly exposed to such stereotypes. Many children's toys are classed either as 'boys' toys' or 'girls' toys' and packaged and marketed accordingly. Through playing with these toys, boys and girls may learn to conform to stereotyped notions of what it means to be a boy or a girl and how they should act. If such stereotypes are reinforced by practitioners, this may lead to increased aggressive and over-assertive behaviour in boys, and more passive behaviour in girls. Practitioners need to guard against such stereotypes, and challenge them when they are in evidence.

Gender stereotyping and discrimination can be resisted by:

◆ encouraging boys to take on caring and nurturing roles during their play;
◆ encouraging girls to take part in construction and physical activities;
◆ making sure that comments such as 'big boys don't cry' are not made when boys are upset;
◆ ensuring that adults provide good role models. For example, female members of staff joining in with football and male members of staff joining in with domestic role-play;

◆ explaining, if necessary, to parents the importance of their son being able to play with dolls or their daughter being able to take part in a game of football;

◆ challenging any sexist remarks that are made and discussing these with the children as appropriate;

◆ having the same expectations of both girls' and boys' behaviour and attainment. If boys are allowed to 'get away with' something that girls are not (or vice versa) this can lead to confusion, resentment and acting out;

◆ not assuming that girls will automatically be 'better behaved' than boys;

◆ having the same rewards and sanctions for both boys' and girls' behaviour;

◆ making sure that particular areas, activities or resources are not dominated by either boys or girls;

◆ not referring to children's gender unnecessarily (e.g. making comments such as 'cheeky boy!' or 'good girl!').

Racial stereotyping and discrimination

From a very early age, children notice differences in skin colour, hair texture and facial features. To begin with, such differences have no particular meaning for children. However, they quickly tune into subtle messages in society and learn to discriminate and stereotype from those around them. For this reason, it is particularly important that early years practitioners provide an anti-discriminatory environment in which stereotypes and discrimination are challenged. As the previous example of the Chinese boy demonstrates, there really are no 'positive' stereotypes. Any attempt to generalise about children on the basis of their racial or cultural group should be resisted.

It is now well-known that African-Caribbean boys are much more likely to be excluded from school than white boys. For example, in 2001 African-Caribbean boys were over three times as likely to be excluded as white boys in secondary schools. Furthermore, in 2003 over 70 per cent of African-Caribbean pupils in London left school with fewer than five or more GCSEs at the top A–C grades (London Development Agency, 2004). As adults, black men are the least likely minority group to have a degree and are twice as likely to be in prison as in university (Holloway, 2004).

From the above, it may seem hard to believe that African-Caribbean boys start their education in early years settings at broadly the same level as other children. By the end of Year 2 (age 7) however, their lower levels of attainment are already apparent (London Development Agency, 2004). It is clear that early years practitioners have an important role to play in ensuring that their minority ethnic children, and in particular black boys, are offered an equitable and non-discriminatory early education that meets their needs and thus maximises their potential for high attainment and appropriate behaviour.

Although well meaning, practitioners who claim to 'treat all children the same' are missing the point, and doing the children in their care a great disservice. Research in the UK and the United States has shown that policies that sought to treat individuals of all ethnic groups the same failed because white professionals tended to have lower expectations of black children. Practitioners need to avoid stereotyping, treating each child according to their individual needs while recognising that some groups face potential disadvantage.

In the research described in the London Development Agency report, African-Caribbean boys reported experiencing both racism and sexism in school. Racism took the forms of being overlooked for answering questions, verbal aggression from teachers and harsher reprimands than for students from other ethnic groups for the same misdemeanour. African-Caribbean boys also expressed concerns about school work not being challenging enough and there not being enough practical or creative activity. Several boys mentioned the damaging effect of labelling black boys as a result of what they wore, who their friends were, how they spoke or whether they had been in trouble before. Many of them felt that the degree of care they received from their teachers, the quality of communication with them and the levels of conflict with them were all less positive for African-Caribbean boys than for boys from other groups.

Although this research has focused on much older children, early years practitioners can learn a great deal from the findings. Given that many African-Caribbean boys have already fallen behind by the age of 7, it seems likely that the issues they raise may be pertinent even in early years settings.

Racial stereotyping and discrimination can be resisted by:

◆ providing positive images and role models for children that confound stereotypes (e.g. making children aware of black scientists and historians as well as athletes and dancers; having books and posters that depict minority ethnic children);
◆ practitioners attending race equality training and other training as necessary (e.g. identifying and responding to racist incidents; creating and devising an inclusive curriculum for minority ethnic children). Such training can often be accessed through LEA Early Years Services and Early Years Development and Childcare Partnerships (EYDCPs);
◆ careful monitoring of rewards, sanctions and responsibilities to ensure that children are not treated differently due to their colour or ethnic group;
◆ challenging and dealing with any racist incidents, whether perpetrated by children, parents or staff;
◆ having high expectations of minority ethnic children's attainment and behaviour;
◆ not mistaking children's assertiveness for 'cheek' or a challenge to authority;
◆ accepting and valuing different accents and ways of speaking rather than correcting children who do not speak 'standard' English;
◆ accepting and valuing different cultural values and parenting styles[1];
◆ being aware of different social norms (e.g. not immediately expecting eye contact from a child who has been taught that it is impolite to look directly at an adult);
◆ not treating minority ethnic children as 'exotic' (e.g. not making comments such as 'Everyone come and look at Sultana! She's wearing a beautiful sari today!');

1 However, it is vital that practitioners take action where they have good reason to suspect child abuse. Recent research suggests that some professionals have been wary of reporting abuse of black or Asian children, fearing that they would be judged to be racist, and justifying their inaction with comments such as 'That's the way they discipline children in their country.'

◆ learning about and celebrating festivals from cultures and religions, but not doing so in a tokenistic way (the 'samosas and saris approach'), and not making assumptions about families' beliefs and cultural practices based solely on their ethnic group.

Other stereotypes

Space precludes detailed discussion of every possible stereotype, but in the same way that gender or racial stereotyping can have a negative effect upon children's attainment and behaviour, stereotyping based upon religion, class, disability, sexuality of parents, socioeconomic status and so on may easily have the same effect. Practitioners should always be mindful of how their own beliefs and prejudices may affect their interactions with the children in the setting, and guard against this.

Maximising positive behaviour through responding to individual needs, learning styles and interests

Much unwanted behaviour results from adults not having given enough thought to providing for children's unique needs. Careful differentiation to match children's learning styles and particular interests is likely to pay dividends in terms of positive behaviour.

While a broadly play-based approach to young children's learning is the best approach for most, practitioners should be aware that their values may differ from those in the child's home. To illustrate this point, research by Liz Brooker at London University's Institute of Education found that some teachers unwittingly discriminated against Bangladeshi children by assuming that a play-based education was equally suitable for all (Brooker, 2002). The Bangladeshi children in Brooker's study arrived at school expecting to 'work', but she concluded that some of them failed to make progress because they thought their teachers wanted them to play. After four months, three of the children had concluded that they were at school to play, and no longer accepted their parents' message that school was about 'work'. They believed that teachers wanted them to play and had not taken in the unspoken message that the aim was to *learn* through play.

The above study demonstrates the importance of taking learning styles into account when planning provision. Children's learning styles may not always be 'innate', and, as in the above example, may also be acquired through their parents' beliefs about education. This does not mean that these children should be given only formal 'work' tasks in their setting, but does suggest that practitioners should take care to explain to both parents and children how learning can also take place through play. If children have been used to more formal learning activities at home, rather than dismissing these, practitioners could offer more structured activities alongside play-based ones so that children feel that what they have learnt at home is valued. If children have been used to highly structured activities at home but are offered only play-based activities in their setting, it is possible that they will become disaffected and begin to behave in unwanted ways. If, however, they are offered a balanced choice of more formal and play-based activities, over time they will learn to appreciate the value of both.

Irrespective of their parents' beliefs about early education, many children have a clearly identifiable learning style linked to one or more senses:

◆ **Visual learners** learn best when information is presented visually. Visual information may take the form of pictures and paintings, photographs, posters, maps, books, video and television, natural objects and artefacts.

◆ **Auditory learners** learn best by hearing information or by associating it with sounds and rhythm. Auditory information may take the form of speaking, songs, chants, rhymes, recorded information (e.g. radio or story-tapes) and music.

◆ **Kinaesthetic learners** learn best by engaging physically with tasks. They learn by acting out the information, story or situation; putting ideas into practice; physical problem-solving; touching and feeling things; holding and manipulating things; and integrating patterns of movement (schemas) into a coherent whole that eventually becomes second nature.

Through careful observation of children both during free play and also while carrying out more structured activities, the astute practitioner can identify children's preferred learning styles. Some children may have more than one learning style. This information can then be used to inform future planning and provision for that child, by exploiting their learning style. If children's learning styles are not taken into account, it is likely that the provision in the setting will not be fully matched to their needs. Ultimately, this may mean that children fail to learn as effectively as they ought, leading to boredom, frustration and unwanted behaviour.

Given that in any group of children, there are likely to be visual, auditory and kinaesthetic learners, skilled practitioners will ensure that they offer a balanced and varied selection of experiences and activities that appeal to children of all learning styles. When a new idea or piece of information is presented to the whole group, the practitioner should make sure that it is presented in a visual way, an auditory way and a kinaesthetic way. For example, when introducing the setting's rules, the rules can be written and illustrated with photographs for visual learners; discussed, recorded, chanted or sung about for auditory learners; and role-played for kinaesthetic learners.

The early years curriculum should also take account of children's personal interests. The foundation stage curriculum is flexible enough to allow a creative response to individual interests, maximising children's enjoyment and achievement, and thus making positive behaviour all the more likely. An example of how this was done in a day nursery is given in *Case study: Alex*, overleaf.

If practitioners are inspired by this case study but concerned that they do not have any money to buy new resources, they should be aware that most of what the nursery did was cost-free. Staff judged the cardboard boxes (thrown away by a local supermarket) to be the most valuable resource of all.

Working with children with language and learning difficulties

It is beyond the scope of this book to go into any great detail about language and learning difficulties in the early years, and there are already a number of good books that cover these areas. However, it is important that practitioners are aware

Case study: Alex

Alex was 3 years old and had been attending a local day nursery for three months. He generally found it difficult to settle to activities, and tended to spend much of the day wandering around the setting. On many occasions he took toys from other children, seemingly simply to provoke a reaction from them. Staff described him as 'mischievous' and 'enjoying taking things from the other children even though he doesn't really want them.' Sometimes Alex would sit on the floor in the outdoor area making train noises, pretending to be a steam train. He could occupy himself in this way for up to half an hour.

When other children's parents started to complain that Alex was upsetting their children, staff decided that they needed to take action. They met with Alex's mother to discuss their concerns. During the meeting, when the train noises were mentioned, she told staff that Alex was 'mad about trains', and spent the vast majority of his time at home either playing with toy trains, looking at books about trains or watching videos about trains.

Alex's nursery didn't have a train set, and when staff checked, they realised that there were no picture books about trains either. Using some money left over from fundraising, they bought a wooden train set and some books about trains. Alex was ecstatic, and, once he had learnt and accepted that the new resources were to be shared, his behaviour improved dramatically. As many of the other children also enjoyed playing with the train set and looking at the books, the staff decided to do a mini-topic about trains. The children made up stories about trains that were scribed by an adult. They then turned their stories into books, using a book-making program on the nursery's computer. The children drew and painted pictures of trains; carried out a survey of whose Mum and Dad went to work on a train; went to watch and count trains passing under a nearby railway bridge; and even made train-shaped biscuits. Their favourite activity of all was making a pretend train from large cardboard boxes in the nursery garden and then 'driving' it around to their favourite places, taking turns (with the support of an adult) to be the train driver.

Staff found that nearly every activity could be given a train focus if they thought creatively enough. When they wanted Alex to do something that didn't involve trains, they used the promise of a train activity later in order to encourage him to take part.

of the impact that such difficulties may have upon children's behaviour. Most practitioners will already be aware that young children with significantly delayed language skills can very easily become frustrated if they are unable to effectively communicate their wants and needs to others. For some children, their behaviour may be the only way they have of communicating what they want or need.

If a child is unable to ask for a turn with a toy, or to verbally protest when another child snatches something from him, it is hardly surprising if that child uses negative physical behaviour to communicate his displeasure. Smacking, pinching and pushing are all very effective ways of saying 'I'm unhappy!' or 'I'm angry!' Of course, these are not behaviours that practitioners would wish to encourage in children, and for this reason, staff must help children to communicate in more acceptable ways. Even a child who is not yet using any words can be taught to tap an adult's arm to attract their attention. Once the child has the adult's attention, he is usually very adept at using gesture and body language to identify which other child has upset him. The adult can check her understanding by asking the child closed questions (e.g. 'Did Sally hurt you/take your toy?'), supplementing speech with mime or gesture as necessary. Nearly all children will be able to confirm whether or not the adult is on the right track with a nod or shake of the head. Other children who witnessed the incident will usually be only to willing to share their version of events, although the 'accused' child will often vehemently deny the allegations! It is important that adults are seen to be fair when dealing with such incidents and should avoid accusing children of misdeeds unless they are absolutely sure of what has happened.

Using gesture, body language and supplementary signing systems such as Makaton can also be very useful strategies to aid children's understanding and thus reduce frustration. Story props, visual timetables, photographs and other visual materials should be used as often as possible to help children with delayed language and learning skills to access the curriculum.

Children at the early stages of learning English as an additional language should not be considered to have language difficulties (unless of course they are also having difficulties in their home language). Bilingualism is an enviable skill. However, the above issues may also apply to young children with English as an additional language until they reach the stage where they can begin to communicate their wants and needs to others. Needless to say, full use should be made of staff, students, parents or volunteers who speak community languages. Children should be made aware of any adults who speak their home language so that they can communicate their wants and needs in their mother tongue. Practitioners may also wish to consider asking parents if they would be willing to translate the setting's rules into children's home languages. It is sensible to double-check any such translations to ensure that they are accurate and worded using positive rather than negative language.

Chapter 5

Teaching emotional literacy

The key to self-esteem and positive behaviour

Young children's emotional development is increasingly recognised as vitally important not only to their attainment but also to their well-being and success in all other areas. Evidence suggests that when social and emotional development are actively targeted in young children, they are more likely to settle into their early years setting, to become confident and co-operative, to know how to behave appropriately in different situations and, in later life, to sustain healthy and balanced relationships. Conversely, when children's social and emotional development is neglected, they are more likely to have difficult relationships with their peers and to have their behaviour described as 'challenging'. Following nationwide inspections in 2003–2004, OFSTED concluded that that the challenging behaviour of many younger children arose mainly as a result of poor language and social skills and poorly developed emotional skills. Research has also demonstrated that children with poor emotional skills run a much greater risk of being involved in crime and experiencing mental health difficulties as adults.

The term *emotional literacy* is increasingly being used to describe the acquisition of skills in this area. The term *emotional intelligence* is often used in the same way, but whereas intelligence is usually thought to be innate and fixed, literacy develops over time. For this reason, emotional literacy is the author's preferred term.

In order to be emotionally literate, individuals need to develop a complex set of attitudes and skills. The skills can be learned, and the attitudes can be adopted, provided that the individual is in an environment that values and nurtures emotional literacy. But what *are* these skills and attitudes? Emotional literacy can be defined as the ability to recognise, understand, deal with and appropriately express emotions, both one's own and those of others. The component skills that make up emotional literacy include:

◆ an ability to reflect upon one's own emotions
◆ self-knowledge (understanding the reasons for one's actions)
◆ an understanding of consequences
◆ self-control

- a healthy self-image (feeling good about oneself, but also being able to acknowledge aspects of oneself that need developing)
- an ability to reflect upon the emotions of others
- an ability to empathise with others
- an understanding of why others behave as they do
- an understanding of how effective relationships are forged and sustained
- an ability to discuss feelings and emotions with others
- a recognition and acceptance of difference and different points of view
- a recognition of the complexity of emotions.

Emotional literacy in early years settings – where do we begin?

An emotionally literate early years setting begins with emotionally literate adults. While most early years teams will get on well together, settings should have a policy of zero-tolerance towards any teasing, name-calling, sarcasm and other negative behaviours that staff may subtly use to undermine another member of the team. There should be regular opportunities (perhaps during staff meetings) to air any issues and grievances in a calm, supportive environment. Staff should provide appropriate emotional support to each other (e.g. through informal peer supervision) when needed. If practitioners are dealing with particularly stressful situations or a child with very disruptive or distressing behaviour, they should 'look out' for each other, arranging staffing so that a member of the team who feels that she needs to take a short unplanned break from the room is able to do so.

Developing children's emotional literacy

Young children have very powerful emotions which often overwhelm them. To begin with, they are unable to name their emotions, much less understand or discuss them. Yet in a typical day, a young child may experience happiness, sadness, fear, anger and a whole range of other emotions, often in quick succession. In early years settings, the practitioner's job is to help children deal with these emotions, particularly negative emotions, in a constructive way, to help children learn to name their emotions, and to teach them how to talk about their feelings.

Children are sensitive to what happens around them, and young children in particular can feel that it is their fault when things go wrong in their setting (such as falling out with a friend). This can make them feel worried and guilty, leading to anxious, withdrawn behaviour. In situations such as these, practitioners have a role to play in talking to children about their feelings and reassuring them.

Not all children's emotions are logical. Young children typically have fears about the dark, insects, monsters and getting lost or abandoned. Such fears are common and normal in all young children. Many children inherit their parents' fears, such as a fear of dogs, through observing their parents' fearful reactions. Usually children grow out of their fears but sometimes they persist as the child grows up – there are many adults who are afraid of spiders or dogs. Again, the practitioner's role is to acknowledge children's feelings, to discuss them as appropriate, and to help them manage their fears.

Talking about feelings

Practitioners should make the most of any opportunity to talk about feelings with children. For example, nearly every children's book is likely to have some emotional content, and there are a number of well-written and illustrated picture books focusing specifically upon emotions. During story-times, adults can explore the emotional content of the books they read, asking children questions such as:

◆   How do you think (the character) feels?
◆   Why does she feel that way?
◆   Have you ever felt like that?
◆   What can she do to make herself feel better?

and so on.

As children develop their emotional vocabulary they should be increasingly encouraged to talk about their feelings. Practitioners can help children learn how

---

Case study: Talking about feelings using self-registration

Staff in the reception class of a Manchester primary school decided to introduce a 'How do I feel today?' self-registration chart as a useful strategy for talking to children about their feelings. The nursery nurse made a large chart on which she drew four large rectangles. Using cartoon drawings from the 'clipart' program on the class computer, a face depicting a different emotion (happy, sad, angry and frightened) was placed in the corner of each rectangle. Self-adhesive Velcro squares were attached to the chart, which was labelled 'How do I feel today?' at the top.

Staff introduced the chart to the class, explaining that each morning, as children arrived, they should think about how they were feeling that day. Next, they should find their name-card (with Velcro on the back) and place it in the appropriate rectangle depending upon how they were feeling. As name-cards had also been made for the staff, they were able to demonstrate how the chart worked.

Children soon got the idea and enjoyed self-registering as they arrived in their class. To begin with, an adult was stationed by the chart to offer help to any child who needed it.

The staff found the chart helpful in two ways. First, it enabled them to immediately see how children were feeling as they arrived in school. Where appropriate, practitioners offered children an immediate opportunity to discuss any negative feelings. Second, during circle time, the self-registration chart was moved over to the carpet area for reference and each child was given the opportunity to explain why they were feeling as they did that day. Over the course of the year, practitioners were pleasantly surprised to discover the extent to which children's ability to talk about and manage their emotions improved through discussing the chart.

to do this by talking about their own feelings – 'I'm feeling happy today because
...'. It is sometimes felt that children should be in some way shielded from
'negative emotions' but it is helpful for the children if practitioners also acknowledge and name their negative feelings. If feeling sad, for example, the practitioner
can explain to the children why she is feeling that way, and talk about the strategies she uses to make herself feel better. It is important that children learn that
there are things they can do to help change the way they feel. Practitioners can
also reassure children that negative feelings usually pass quite quickly.

The strategy in *Case study: Talking about feelings* can be adapted to meet the
needs of different settings. The emotions *happy*, *sad*, *angry* and *frightened* were
chosen because they are very common feelings in young children and are comparatively easy to understand. Settings may wish to begin by simply giving children
a choice of *happy* and *sad*. As children become more adept at recognising and
naming their feelings, additional choices could be introduced. Instead of name-
cards, photographs can be used for children who are not yet able to recognise their
own name. Many settings find that a feelings chart is a good activity for parents
to share with their child as they arrive. Obviously, it is important that children are
allowed to decide for themselves how they are feeling, rather than being told by
their parents. Practitioners should be sensitive to parents' own feelings where children self-register a 'negative' emotion, and if necessary reassure them that this
does not reflect badly upon their parenting.

If such a chart is to be discussed during circle time (or 'emotional literacy time'),
useful questions to ask the children include:

◆ Why were you feeling that way when you arrived today?
◆ Are you still feeling that way?
◆ If not, how are you feeling now?
◆ What has made you change the way you feeling?
◆ If you're still feeling (a negative emotion), what could you do to help you feel
   better?
◆ What can the rest of us do to help you feel better?
◆ What do the rest of us do when we're feeling (a negative emotion)?
◆ What things make us feel that way?
◆ What things make us feel better?

Using puppets

Puppets can be a particularly useful resource to support the teaching of emotional
literacy skills. Good quality puppets immediately attract young children's attention
and hold their interest. Puppets can be used to act out scenarios that directly repre-
sent situations and relationships within a setting without making them too personal
or blaming individuals. This can avoid children feeling self-conscious, embarrassed
or victimised. Children can also practise expressing feelings towards a puppet in
a non-threatening way, for example, being given the choice of a smile, a wave or a
kiss to say goodbye to the puppet.

Practitioners sometimes worry that they would be 'no good' at using puppets
with the children. They may argue that they are unable to do different voices

for the puppets, or make them do complex moves. However, this is really not necessary; young children are a very accepting audience and do not expect expert puppetry. On the contrary, they are more than willing to suspend disbelief and enter into the puppets' world.

All adults in the setting should have a shared understanding of each puppet's history and circumstances and maintain this (e.g. name, likes and dislikes). This will make the puppet a believable personality that the children can better relate to. Puppets used by adults in a setting for emotional literacy or circle time sessions should be kept solely for this purpose and not be available to the children to play with. Children should have access to smaller, visually dissimilar puppets for their own free play.

Emotional literacy scenarios for puppets

Puppets may be used by practitioners to enact any scenario or explore any feeling. Issues and events that have taken place or are about to take place in the setting can be enacted using the puppets, and their emotional content explored. Such scenarios can be a very useful way of discussing negative emotions and helping children to think about how the events that lead to these emotions can be dealt with. In turn, children learn about how to manage their feelings in a constructive way.

Puppet scenarios of this type are not difficult to create, and while it is obviously a good idea for staff to practice them with the puppets before introducing them to the children, they need not worry about being word-perfect. Provided that the emotion is dealt with in a way that is accessible to the children, it does not matter if practitioners deviate from the script. An example is given below to show how such scenarios may be structured.

Puppet scenario: Name-calling

Props – Two child puppets

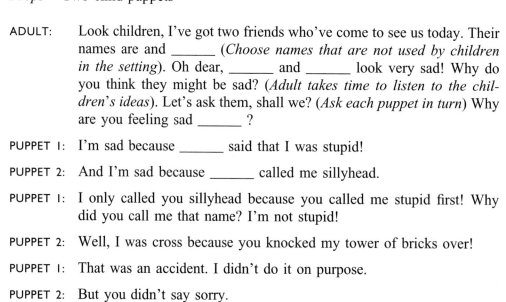

ADULT: Look children, I've got two friends who've come to see us today. Their names are and _____ (*Choose names that are not used by children in the setting*). Oh dear, _____ and _____ look very sad! Why do you think they might be sad? (*Adult takes time to listen to the children's ideas*). Let's ask them, shall we? (*Ask each puppet in turn*) Why are you feeling sad _____ ?

PUPPET 1:   I'm sad because _____ said that I was stupid!

PUPPET 2:   And I'm sad because _____ called me sillyhead.

PUPPET 1:   I only called you sillyhead because you called me stupid first! Why did you call me that name? I'm not stupid!

PUPPET 2:   Well, I was cross because you knocked my tower of bricks over!

PUPPET 1:   That was an accident. I didn't do it on purpose.

PUPPET 2:   But you didn't say sorry.

PUPPET 1:   Well, I am sorry I knocked your tower over.

PUPPET 2:   And I'm sorry I called you stupid.

PUPPET 1:   And I'm sorry I called you sillyhead. Let's be friends again.

PUPPET 2:   OK. Let's go and build another tower together!

ADULT: Well I'm glad that's sorted out. Well done _____ and _____ for apologising to each other. (*Ask the children if anyone has ever called them names. How did they feel? What did they do? What should they do if someone calls them names? Talk to the children about how name-calling is hurtful and discuss more acceptable ways of dealing with anger or frustration.*)

Similar scenarios can easily be created for issues such as not being allowed to join in with a game, snatching toys, fighting, being frightened of something, or any of the other things that children may have difficulty with.

Strategies for helping children express anger

Anger is a natural human emotion that all adults and children will experience from time to time. Children need to learn how to express this powerful, often frightening, emotion in a safe way, as uncontrolled anger can be very destructive.

Young children need to learn:

◆ how to recognise feelings of anger
◆ how to express anger without hurting other children or adults or destroying property
◆ how to control impulses aroused when angry
◆ how to calm themselves
◆ how to express angry feelings in a positive way
◆ how to resolve the problem or issue that caused the anger
◆ how to separate themselves from violent or angry events
◆ how to seek support from adults, if needed, to help them deal with their anger.

Useful strategies

Helping children learn to relax

When young children are angry, the emotion creates physical responses within the body. Heart rate may increase, muscles may become tense and the stomach may ache. Practitioners can help children to identify these responses and to relax. One of the most effective ways of coping with these unwanted physical responses to anger is to do something else physical.

Children can calm their anger through activities that involve one or more of the senses. Appropriate activities might include painting, squashing dough, running around, listening to music, slow deep breathing, eating a healthy snack or stroking or hugging a soft toy.

The practitioner might say:

- 'Shall we go and run really fast together outside until you feel better?'
- 'Perhaps you could paint a picture about your feelings.'
- 'Sit down and take slow breaths until you are calm.'

Helping children learn to communicate

Young children can learn to communicate anger in various ways. Children who have sufficient language skills may be able to talk about things with a caring adult or a friend. A soft toy may also be a good listener.

A child may become very angry but not be able to tell a practitioner why, as her language and thinking skills are not yet sufficiently well-developed. Often young children need to be given the words to get what they want, to be able to join in or to stand up for themselves. Staff can help children by encouraging them to practice appropriate phrases.

The practitioner might say:

- 'Say to Farhad, "Can I play too?"'
- 'Say to him, "When I've finished you can have a turn."'
- 'Tell Sonia, "I won't play if you keep calling me names."'
- 'Ask a grown-up if you need help.'
- 'Tell a grown-up before you lose control.'

Helping children learn to solve problems

Practitioners should help children to identify solutions to the situations they face that may make them feel angry. Over time the children will become more able to come up with their own solutions.

The practitioner might say:

- 'Stop. I see two children getting very angry. Let's try and solve the problem together.'
- 'Listen to each other to find out how each person feels about this.'
- 'What's wrong?'
- 'How can the rest of us help to sort this out?'
- 'Did the idea work well?'
- 'What might work better next time?'

Helping children learn to change the environment

If feelings are getting out of control it is often best if children are able to remove themselves from the situation until the feelings have subsided. Practitioners should identify places where it is safe to do this within their setting (such as a nurture corner), both inside and outside.

The practitioner might say:

◆ 'When things feel wrong it is OK to walk away.'
◆ 'Do you think it would be a good idea to spend some time away from Paul?'
◆ 'Cool down and take a break.'

Give children alternatives

Telling a child what *not* to do is always best followed up with a suggestion of something they *can* do. For example:

You may not . . .	But you may . . .
Hit someone	Tell them that they have made you feel angry
Hurt yourself	Squeeze a stress ball
Bite someone	Talk about things with a grown-up
Break something	Rip up old newspaper
Yell or scream at someone	Go outside and shout at the sky

Chapter 6

Positive observation and record keeping

Monitoring children's progress across the curriculum and having accurate and effective record keeping systems that inform future planning is clearly an important part of any early years practitioner's role. Devising systems that are manageable can be a challenge, given the ever-increasing demands on practitioners' time. Rather than being seen as somehow separate from the foundation stage curriculum, children's behaviour should be given its rightful place at the heart of the personal, social and emotional area of learning. Behaviour cannot be considered in isolation, and practitioners need to be aware of how it links to all other areas of the curriculum. Behaviour strongly influences, and is influenced by, children's progress in all six areas of learning.

Careful observation is an important way of monitoring children's progress in all areas, including their behaviour. However, when observing children with behaviour in mind, many practitioners tend to focus upon unwanted behaviours. By only focusing upon children's unwanted behaviour, improvements are less likely to occur. Negative attention tends to reinforce unwanted or unacceptable behaviour. A positive approach to observation looks at children's behaviour as a whole – both the positive and the less positive aspects of their behaviour. Thoughtful practitioners will be aware that behaviour is always used to communicate, and will always try to work out the message that the child is communicating through his behaviour. Reflective practitioners will also monitor their own behaviour – How did I respond to x today? How did I respond to y? Why did x happen more than y? Was it due to my own behaviour?

If a number of children are observed to engage in a particular behaviour – either a positive or an unwanted behaviour – then this tells the practitioner that the environment is likely to be responsible for that behaviour, and not some 'within-child' characteristic. The environmental factor might be the adult's own behaviour, the organisation of the curriculum or the layout of the room. By thinking about possible environmental reasons for children's behaviours rather than locating the behaviour 'within-child', the practitioner is taking the first step towards being able to change the environment, and so encourage more positive behaviour.

The ABC approach to observing children's behaviour

One potentially useful way to think about children's behaviour has its roots in behavioural psychology and is often referred to as the ABC approach. This approach is generally used to think about unwanted behaviours in children, but it can also be used to good effect when considering more positive behaviours.

A stands for antecedents

Antecedent is a term used to describe the things that precede the behaviour in question. Antecedents may be specific actions or events, but the term also refers to the contextual and causal factors of behaviour, such as the setting's organisation, the practitioners' own behaviour or the way in which language is used. The antecedents can be thought of as the things that trigger a particular behaviour and the situations in which it happens.

Practitioners should consider:

◆ *Where* the behaviour happens. For example: 'Georgia usually has temper tantrums in the role-play area' or 'Amir is usually very helpful at tidy-up time.'
◆ *When* it happens. For example: 'Tom always screams when it's lunchtime' or 'Shereen is generally much happier in the morning.'
◆ *Who* is there. For example: 'Bobby seems to find it difficult to play with Steven' or 'Sultana never screams when Dad takes her to school.'

B stands for behaviour

When thinking about the behaviour in question, whether positive or negative, it is important to be able to describe this clearly. For example, the statement 'Wayne is very disobedient' is not only a very negative way of describing Wayne that makes a sweeping generalisation about his behaviour, it is also a very unclear statement. If, on the other hand, the statement is changed to 'Wayne runs away when I call him', it is clear exactly which behaviour is of concern.

In considering the child's behaviour, the following prompts may be useful:

◆ How is unwanted, unacceptable or destructive behaviour expressed?
◆ What is the goal of that behaviour: is it attention seeking, demonstrating power, seeking power, or is it task avoidance?

C stands for consequences

Any behaviour, positive or otherwise, will have consequences. The consequences of a child's behaviour may have the effect a child was seeking, or may be completely at odds with expectations. Hopefully, the consequence of a positive behaviour, such as sharing a toy with another child, will also be positive; for example, the child is praised by a practitioner or receives a smile from the other child. Unfortunately, positive behaviour does not always have a positive consequence; the practitioner may be so focused upon dealing with unwanted behaviour that she fails to notice and praise the positive. Clearly, such behaviour is less likely to happen again if the child does not see the consequence as positive. For this reason, when monitoring children's behaviour, practitioners should always aim to ensure that positive behaviours are acknowledged and positively reinforced.

The consequences of inappropriate behaviour may result in extreme and difficult situations, or the consequences may be fairly minor. Consequences follow for both practitioners and children. If the consequence of inappropriate behaviour was rewarding for the child (e.g. gaining attention), then she is likely to repeat that behaviour. Many children prefer negative attention to no attention at all.

In considering the consequences of a child's behaviour, the following prompts may be useful:

◆   How can you as a practitioner influence those consequences?
◆   Will there be a desired and successful outcome to the actions you take?

For example:

◆   Are you rewarding with a smile or a word of praise the behaviour you want to encourage?
◆   Or are you giving a lot of attention to what you want to discourage?

Applying the ABC model in early years settings

The underlying approach of the ABC model is to address the antecedents – the factors within the setting that lead to the behaviour in question. The emphasis is on the belief that by addressing the antecedents to behaviour, the practitioner focuses upon contextual issues that can be addressed through effective practice.

Practitioners should first identify a particular behaviour they wish to focus upon. This may be an unwanted behaviour that they are hoping to address. Having identified this behaviour, practitioners should then think about the antecedents to that behaviour, asking the questions *where*, *when* and *who with*? Finally, practitioners should consider the consequences of the behaviour, for them, the child in question and any other children present.

Following this process, the practitioner should aim to change the antecedents and/or the consequences in order to make positive behaviour more likely to occur in future.

Practitioners may also choose to focus upon a positive behaviour using the ABC model, as it is clearly invaluable to gain a better understanding of the factors (antecedents) that lead to positive behaviour. In this case, once a practitioner

Case study part 1: Ella

Ella was happy in her nursery and her behaviour was generally positive. However, she did not like tidy-up times, and usually continued to play with toys while the other children tidied up. If asked to stop, she generally ignored the request, and then, as a practitioner approached, ran off into a different area of the setting. This often resulted in the adult following her in an attempt to get the toy and persuade her to go back to the main room.

has identified antecedents and consequences, the aim would be for her to ensure that these antecedents are in place as often as possible, leading to more instances of the desired behaviour. The practitioner should also check that the consequences are appropriate, as they will go on to be the antecedents for future behaviour.

Case study part 1: Ella shows how the ABC model can be applied to a particular issue.

Using the ABC model, the above case study can be represented as follows:

Antecedent	Behaviour	Consequence
Ella is playing. The children are asked to tidy up.	Ella continues to play, and then takes her toy and runs away.	An adult follows in pursuit.

In this case, Ella found the consequence of her behaviour rewarding. She enjoyed running away from the adult and perceived this as a chasing game. By the time she had been 'caught' or persuaded back into the main area the room had usually been tidied, meaning that Ella successfully avoided the task.

Case study part 2: Ella

Staff realised that Ella's behaviour at tidy-up time was not likely to change while she was effectively being rewarded for refusing to join in with tidying-up. They decided to make the following changes:

◆ The children were given five minutes' warning before tidy-up time to prepare them for this transition.
◆ Staff told children that if they tidied-up quickly, there would be time for a game before lunch or home time. Children who tidied-up particularly well were allowed to choose the game.
◆ Staff gave verbal encouragement to Ella to tidy-up, but did not pursue her if she ran away with her toy.
◆ Once the other children had finished tidying-up, they played a fun game.
◆ Ella was able to join the game as soon as she had put away her toy(s). An adult was on hand to help if necessary.

Case study part 2: Ella can be represented as follows:

Antecedent	Behaviour	Consequence
Ella is given five minutes' warning before tidy-up time and reminded about	Ella tidies away her toy(s).	Ella gets to choose a chasing game that she and all the other children love.
the game that will take place once children	Ella continues to play with her toy(s) and	Ella is not involved in the chasing game.

Antecedent	Behaviour	Consequence
have tidied-up. Ella is given personal encouragement to tidy-up.	does not tidy them away.	If she tries to join in, she is not stopped, but the chaser (a practitioner) will not choose her to chase until she has put her toy(s) away, meaning that the game is no fun for Ella.

Clearly, the reward of choosing a chasing game was by far the best consequence for Ella, and she quickly began to adjust her behaviour accordingly and tidied-up her toy(s).

Positive record keeping

Finding time for record keeping can be a challenge, and to ensure that precious time is not wasted, practitioners may wish to ask themselves the following questions:

- Do I need to write this down?
- What is the purpose of this record?
- How will this record inform future practice?

As with any other area, when recording children's behaviour, the practitioner should aim to record only what she judges to be significant. Of course, it is not always easy to decide what is significant, particularly when first thinking about a child's behaviour. However, the practitioner should guard against writing down every minor infringement of the setting's rules. When recording observations, it is particularly important that practitioners write down what the child actually did (i.e. the behaviour itself) rather than their subjective interpretation of this.

Write down the behaviour itself . . .	**Not** your subjective interpretation of it
'John went over to Britney and took the doll she was playing with from her.'	'John was in a bad mood today and snatched Britney's doll from her for no reason other than to upset her.'
'Alice spent half an hour running in large circles around the playground this morning.'	'Alice was completely hyper this morning and ran around like a whirlwind. She's obviously been cooped up indoors all weekend.'

The interpretation can come later, after careful thought has been given to antecedents and consequences. Where practitioners do have ideas about why children may have behaved in a particular way, it is a good idea to check these out with colleagues and parents – Have they noticed the same thing? Do they agree with your interpretation?

Unfortunately, it is still the case that many schools have 'behaviour books' or 'incident books' that are filled with examples of unacceptable behaviour. Where are the examples of good behaviour (which will undoubtedly outnumber the incidences of bad behaviour several times over) recorded? Do we really believe that only 'bad' behaviour is noteworthy? If this is the case, with all the attention given to unwanted behaviours, it is hardly surprising that children repeat them. If settings do feel that it is necessary to have an incident book, they should also have a 'good behaviour book' in which they record as many examples of positive behaviour as possible. Children should be made aware of the good behaviour book, and practitioners should share its contents with the group on a regular basis.

Over the course of a month (or more regularly if feasible), practitioners should observe all children, not only the ones deemed to have inappropriate behaviour. Where staff are particularly challenged by the behaviour of a certain child, they should give that child a break from their observations, to allow them to keep things in perspective. The child in question will also undoubtedly know that he is being scrutinised, which could possibly lead to an escalation in his unwanted behaviours. If there are 'victims' on the receiving end of a child's behaviour, it is important that they too are observed, in order to shed light on antecedents to the behaviour. At times, practitioners may discover that the 'victim' has actually provoked the target child.

When recording observations, practitioners should avoid generalisations such as 'Zoe always fights with the other children'. Using words such as *always*, *constantly* and *never* to describe the frequency of particular behaviours is inaccurate and unhelpful. Instead, practitioners should note the number of times or length of time a child engaged in that behaviour. For obvious reasons, staff should avoid words such as *bad*, *naughty*, *disgraceful* or *spiteful* when describing children's behaviour.

Practitioners must avoid concluding 'He did it for no reason'. Just because the practitioner has not been able to identify why a child behaved as he did, it does not mean that the child's actions were random and meaningless. However concerned staff may be about a child's behaviour, they should always remember to record the wanted behaviour as well as the unwanted. In the same way that practitioners will aim to 'catch the child being good', they may sometimes decide that they will only record a child's positive behaviour that day (unless something serious happens that absolutely must be put in writing) and aim to write at least a page of positive observations. Practitioners should always remember that a true understanding of the child comes from their focusing not only on unwanted behaviours, but also on the child's good behaviour. Positive observation and record keeping systems will support practitioners' efforts to increase children's good behaviour and minimise that which is unwanted.

Chapter 7

Working in partnership with parents to promote positive behaviour

Earlier chapters hopefully show just how vital it is to have a good working relationship with parents. In the introduction, the pitfalls of blaming parents for their children's behaviour were highlighted. Chapter 1 discussed the importance of sharing information between practitioners and parents, the benefits of home visiting and the role of parents in settling their child into a setting. This chapter will examine in more detail how practitioners and parents can work together to support positive behaviour in children.

What does 'working in partnership with parents' actually mean?

The importance of parental involvement in children's education has long been recognised. For more than twenty years, a series of research and development programmes have consistently shown a range of benefits and positive outcomes that derive from the active encouragement and involvement of parents in their children's learning. Parents who value education and convey their values through enthusiasm and positive parenting have a great impact upon their children's self-perception as learners, their motivation, self-esteem and educational aspirations. In turn, confident, motivated children with healthy self-esteem are much more likely to display more of the behaviour that the practitioner wishes to see, and less unwanted behaviour.

In recent years, the term 'parental partnership' has become increasingly popular. This term extends the idea of parental involvement into a partnership model, in which both parents and practitioners have rights and responsibilities. The word *partnership* implies a relationship in which there are shared goals. This highlights the importance of practitioners sharing their policies and practices with parents, ensuring that parents understand what the setting is aiming to achieve, and why. Without this shared understanding, true partnership between practitioners and parents is impossible.

The word partnership also suggests a relationship in which both sides are equal. However, in the context of early years education, this may be problematic. Some parents may feel disempowered or intimidated by the education system, even in the relatively parent-friendly early years sector. Parents who have had negative experiences in their own education may find that such experiences adversely affect how they think about the provision for their own children. Some parents may not be able, or may not wish, to be heavily involved in their child's early years setting, but this does not mean that they will not be supporting their child's learning and behaviour at home. Any partnership model needs to be flexible in order to meet the needs of all parents, and should aim to minimise the effects of inequality.

The table on pp. 60–61 summarises some of the rights and responsibilities of parents and practitioners, based upon a partnership model, focusing in particular upon behaviour.

In an ideal partnership, both practitioners and parents would fulfil all of their responsibilities and have all of their rights satisfied at all times. Of course, the ideal may not always match the reality, but this should not be used as an excuse to abandon the partnership. For example, a parent not fulfilling his responsibilities does not give the practitioner the right to abandon her own responsibilities in relation to that parent and his child. Practitioners should always be thinking about how to overcome any obstacles in order to strengthen partnership with parents. Comments such as 'Joe's Mum couldn't care less' should always be challenged, as they are unhelpful and almost certainly inaccurate. There are many different reasons why a parent may appear not to be fulfilling all of her parental responsibilities, but the practitioner's role is not to speculate upon parents' commitment. Instead, practitioners should ask: 'What can we do to encourage Joe's Mum to work more closely with us?'

Home–setting agreements and parental partnership policies

The idea of a home–setting agreement began in schools, where such documents were conceived as a way of making the rights and responsibilities of both parents and staff absolutely clear. A home–setting agreement is a written document that sets out exactly what parents can expect from the setting, and what the setting can expect from parents. The document is usually signed by both parties to demonstrate their commitment to the agreement. Sykes (2001) found that parents expressed overwhelmingly positive views about the process and outcome of home–school agreements. Many of the parents involved were from minority ethnic groups, and Sykes suggested that the process was particularly helpful to them in that it initiated consultation and helped to clarify issues concerning their child's learning.

Such agreements are now being introduced in early years settings, and it seems reasonable to assume that the benefits that Sykes described in schools will also apply to early years settings. A well-written agreement should help to clarify parents' understanding of what the setting is aiming to achieve both in terms of children's learning and their behaviour.

If settings decide to introduce a home–setting agreement, it should be made absolutely clear to parents that they are not being asked to sign a legally binding document. Some schools and settings have referred to such agreements as 'contracts', which is potentially misleading and off-putting. For moral reasons, parents should not be led to believe that such 'contracts' are legally enforceable,

Rights	*Responsibilities*
Parents	
◆ To expect that practitioners will treat their child fairly and positively, and that any sanctions taken will be proportionate.	◆ To encourage their child to behave appropriately, establishing and reinforcing clear boundaries.
◆ To be kept informed about their child's behaviour and informed immediately that there are any concerns.	◆ To act as a good role model for positive behaviour.
◆ To expect to be spoken to constructively about their child's behaviour, and not to have their child labelled.	◆ Where possible, to inform setting staff of any incidents or circumstances that may impact upon their child's behaviour.
◆ To be given appropriate opportunities to share insights and ideas to support their child's behaviour in the setting.	◆ To discuss with the child and address any incidents that have taken place in their child's setting.
◆ Where requested, to be given advice on strategies to encourage positive behaviour at home.	◆ To listen to practitioners' points of view and consider implementing any suggestions made in relation to behaviour.
◆ To have their views listened to and acknowledged.	
◆ To expect that practitioners will take account of and respect any cultural differences that may impact upon children's behaviour.	

Practitioners	
◆ To expect high standards for behaviour.	◆ To make expectations in relation to behaviour absolutely clear to parents (e.g. through the setting's behaviour policy).
◆ To expect that parents will support them in promoting positive behaviour.	
◆ To be spoken to politely and calmly by parents when discussing a child's behaviour.	◆ To share any concerns about children's behaviour promptly with parents, sensitively and constructively.
◆ To have their views listened to and acknowledged.	◆ To act as a good role model for positive behaviour.

Rights	Responsibilities
◆ To be able to access support from others when intervening in children's behaviour (e.g. SENCO, headteacher, nursery manager, Local Education Authority).	◆ To treat all children fairly. ◆ To use positive behaviour strategies. ◆ To keep up-to-date with theory and practice in relation to children's behaviour. ◆ To take into account and respect any cultural differences that may impact upon children's behaviour.

and that their child could be excluded if they are 'in breach of contract'. The document need not necessarily be signed, and could simply be given to parents (following discussion to check their understanding of and commitment to the agreement) and displayed in the setting as a reminder of what both parties have committed to. Practitioners should bear in mind the potential effect of asking parents with literacy difficulties to sign something that they are unable to read. Hopefully, the vast majority of parents will see the agreement as a positive tool and will be only too happy to declare their allegiance to it.

Settings committed to true partnership may wish to consider setting up a working party with parents to draft a home–setting agreement. In this way, parents become key stakeholders in the process and can claim equal ownership of the agreement. Furthermore, discussion and debate arising from the establishment of a working party would give both parents and staff an opportunity to clarify their values and aims, developing a shared understanding of children's learning and behaviour which would underpin effective partnership.

Sykes' research suggests that, for minority ethnic parents unfamiliar with early years education in the UK, an agreement that has been properly discussed and disseminated is likely to help parents understand the childcare and early education systems and to appreciate the goals of the setting. A properly introduced home–setting agreement may be a useful tool in widening the participation of traditionally disenfranchised groups and contributing to effective partnership with parents.

A sample behaviour section from a home–setting agreement can be found in Appendix 3 of this book.

The home–setting agreement idea could be further extended into a parental partnership policy. Settings have an ever-increasing number of policies, but very few have an explicit policy on working with parents. Some settings have inclusion policies that may outline a commitment to working in partnership with parents, but a dedicated parental partnership policy could describe in detail how that commitment is put into practice. The development of a parental partnership policy would provide an invaluable opportunity for joint working and debate with parents. A policy which is jointly owned by staff and parents is arguably more likely to be a dynamic tool that is implemented on a daily basis, rather than a document that gathers dust on a shelf.

Making time for parents

When parents do not work or study, it is usually relatively easy to find time to meet with them to discuss their child's progress and any concerns they may have. However, where parents work, particularly full-time, it is often difficult to meet with them face-to-face. Communicating with parents via written correspondence can be effective, but this should not be the only form of communication between home and setting.

Home–setting contact books can be a useful way of sharing information about what children have been doing at home and in the setting. However, such books are not really suitable for communicating concerns about children's behaviour. Understandably, parents will wish to discuss such concerns in person, and may be left feeling anxious if their only channel of communication is through a contact book. Such books also assume that parents have a certain level of literacy, whereas some parents may find it difficult to read what has been written about their child. A contact book also implies an expectation that the parent will make a written response to the entries made by setting staff. This may create anxiety on the part of parents who are not confident in their own writing skills or who have little time to compose a written response.

Some parents may be able to take time off work to discuss their child with setting staff, but this should not be an expectation. Taking time off work may cause considerable inconvenience to some parents; depending upon their job, the time taken off may be unpaid, or they may be expected to make up for lost productivity in their own time. Some parents may understandably feel uncomfortable about asking for time off to discuss their child's behaviour, and may feel compelled to give another reason for asking for time off.

It is far preferable if setting staff are able to be flexible about when they offer appointments to parents. Early morning or evening appointments should be offered to working parents wherever possible. If staff do not usually work at these times, it will hopefully be possible for them to be given time off in lieu rather than relying on practitioners' good will. Of course, if practitioners have fixed working hours, they cannot be required to work at other times, but it is hoped that settings will recognise the benefits of a flexible approach and will make every effort to offer flexible meeting times. Where this is not possible (for example, where practitioners have commitments such as collecting their own children from school), parents should be given opportunities to communicate with staff on the telephone, or via another mutually convenient method.

Discussing children's behaviour with parents in a positive way

Parents may well feel apprehensive about the idea of a meeting to discuss their child's behaviour. The solution to this is simple: practitioners should never invite parents to meetings solely to talk about their child's behaviour. Behaviour is best understood in the context of the child's overall progress and development, and so parents should be invited to a meeting to discuss their child's progress. Even if it is just the child's behaviour that has prompted a meeting, there will undoubtedly also be many positive things to discuss with parents. If parents ask: 'Is it about his behaviour?' practitioners should be honest and say that behaviour is one of the areas that will be discussed, among others.

Pointers for a positive meeting

◆ Practitioners should make sure that there is adequate time for the meeting, and agree with parents at the beginning how much time each party has and by what time the meeting needs to finish.
◆ Parents have a right to expect privacy for such meetings. Practitioners should arrange a meeting place that allows privacy and no interruptions.
◆ The meeting place should be comfortable and parents should ideally be offered light refreshments to help make them feel welcome.
◆ Arrange the seating informally (e.g. three chairs in a triangle arrangement). If the practitioner sits facing parents behind a desk it can create the impression that they are being interviewed or interrogated.
◆ Even where the child's behaviour is of serious concern, practitioners should *always* start the meeting by talking about some of the positive aspects of his progress and development.
◆ When discussing concerns, practitioners should keep to the facts, describing incidents clearly but avoiding labelling the child's behaviour. If the practitioner interprets the child's behaviour, she should be prepared to explain her reasoning and to check parents' own perceptions.
◆ Practitioners should use active listening skills, including:
  – using positive body language such as smiling and nodding
  – checking that they have understood what parents are saying
  – paraphrasing
  – returning to an issue to clarify their understanding
  – asking for more information or detail or elaboration
  – acknowledging feelings
  – empathising
  – affirming the positive.
◆ Where there is a difference of opinion, practitioners should respect parents' views while reiterating the reasoning behind their own views. Rather than becoming confrontational, it is usually better to 'agree to disagree'.
◆ Practitioners should aim to finish the meeting on a positive note by reiterating strengths and positive aspects of the child.
◆ Practitioners should ensure that parents are clear about what will happen next as a result of the meeting. It should be clear who is to do what.

Responding to parents' requests for help

From time to time, parents may ask practitioners for help in managing their child's behaviour. Practitioners should not underestimate how much courage it can take for some parents to make such a request. They may feel inadequate and that they are failing in their parental duties. Sensitive practitioners will offer reassurance that parenting can be a difficult task, and clarify exactly what support the parent needs.

Where the child's behaviour is not of concern within the setting, practitioners can reassure parents that it is not uncommon for children to behave differently in different settings, and that it does not necessarily mean that the parent is 'doing something wrong'. The parent should be given detailed information about the strategies that are used in the setting to promote positive behaviour, and encouraged to try these at home. Practitioners should emphasise the importance of a consistent approach. Parents could be invited to come into the setting and watch how staff use positive behaviour strategies in their day-to-day practice, but should be aware that their child might well behave differently in the presence of her mother or father.

Where practitioners judge that a parent is having serious difficulties parenting their child, it may be appropriate to involve external support agencies. All local authorities are likely to have some form of parenting skills training, whether this is provided by social services, the education department or through local Children's Centres. All parenting training will include an element of 'behaviour management', and some authorities may run courses for parents focusing specifically on behaviour. Practitioners may wish to consider inviting parents to any behaviour training that they themselves are accessing. Even training designed specifically for early years practitioners will include much that is useful to parents.

Practitioners should obviously use their professional judgement and be sensitive to parents' feelings when suggesting the involvement of an external agency. If parents do not wish to have this type of involvement, practitioners should respect their views, and avoid making negative assumptions about the parents' commitment to parenting. Only when practitioners have good reason to suspect abuse or a serious risk of abuse should an external agency (i.e. social services) be contacted against the parents' wishes. In this case, parents *must* be informed (except in the case of sexual abuse) that a referral is being made. Practitioners may judge that such referrals will seriously compromise partnership with parents, but in situations such as these, taking no action is not an option.

Cultural considerations

To a certain extent, norms for children's behaviour are culturally bound, and what is considered to be appropriate behaviour may vary considerably between different cultures. This fact highlights the benefits of well-written behaviour policies and home–setting agreements that are shared with parents. All parents need to understand what the setting expects in terms of children's behaviour and why. Practitioners should feel confident in outlining what constitutes acceptable behaviour for their setting, provided of course that they are able to justify each of their behaviour rules. However, in doing so, they should avoid giving parents the impression that the standards of behaviour they expect in the setting are exactly the same as those that should be applied in the child's home. Nor should they give the impression that parents' rules are in some way inferior to the setting's rules. Provided that parental expectations and interventions in behaviour are within the law, it is not for the practitioner to judge them to be inappropriate. However, it is perfectly reasonable for practitioners to expect that parents will conform to the setting's standards for behaviour while in the setting (e.g. no smacking of children).

Parents volunteering in the setting

Clearly, all parents should be made to feel welcome in the setting and should be invited to join in fully in the life of the setting. This includes parents 'helping out' in the setting, which might take the form of joining in with activities with children, assisting with administrative tasks or being involved in fundraising. While such participation is to be welcomed and has been shown to be of benefit to parents as well as the setting, parents should not feel that this type of direct participation is expected of them. Some parents will be unable to 'help out' due to work or other commitments, while others may, for one reason or another, not wish to be involved in this way. Practitioners should not assume that this means that parents are not committed to their child's childcare and early education.

Research has demonstrated that the most significant factor in children's success is 'at-home good parenting' (Desforges and Abouchaar, 2003). As stated earlier, any model of parental partnership needs to be flexible in order to meet the needs of all parents. The key to effective partnership is a shared understanding and commitment to common goals; for some parents this will include a substantial amount of direct participation in the life of the setting, while other parents will contribute to the partnership through their 'at-home good parenting'. Both forms of participation should be seen as equally valid.

Any parents who do 'help out' in the setting should, as part of their induction, be informed of policy and practice in relation to children's behaviour. This would include:

◆ the importance of maintaining confidentiality around behaviour issues, i.e. not telling other parents that 'Joanne was a handful today';
◆ the importance of a consistent approach among all adults in relation to behaviour issues. If parents do not feel confident in dealing with issues that arise, they should feel able to inform a member of staff;
◆ the importance of treating their own children in the same way as any other, neither favouring them nor treating them less favourably;
◆ making sure that parents appreciate that their presence may cause their own children to 'act up' and that they know how to deal with this;
◆ making sure that parents use appropriate language when talking to children about their behaviour.

Chapter 8

Positive strategies for working with particular groups of children

The vast majority of strategies for maximising positive behaviour will work well with most young children. This book has, wherever possible, sought to avoid labelling children based upon their behaviour. However, there are some groups of children for whom an appreciation of their particular difficulties is essential in informing positive behaviour strategies. This chapter contains sections on working with children with autism, children with attention difficulties (including those with a formal diagnosis of ADHD) and children who are withdrawn or very distressed. It is beyond the scope of this book to go into detail about these conditions; there are many good books available that focus exclusively on such difficulties. Instead, this chapter will offer some strategies that will support positive behaviour in these groups of children. It is expected that practitioners will also seek advice and support from outside professionals such as educational psychologists, therapists and specialist teachers.

Labels such as 'autistic' or 'child with ADHD' *can* be helpful to parents and practitioners alike. For parents, once they have overcome their initial shock and distress, a diagnosis can almost be a relief: many parents report always having known that something was 'not right', and may feel comforted that they can at last put a name to their child's condition. Of course, much is still unknown about conditions such as autism. Having the label 'autistic' helps us to understand to a certain extent why a child behaves as he does, and to predict how he might behave in future. However, we do not yet know what causes autism, nor *why* children with autism have difficulties with social communication. Thus a statement such as 'He behaves like that because he's autistic' can never fully explain the child's behaviour.

With any label, the danger is that people will have very rigid expectations (often low expectations) of the child, and will focus on the condition at the expense of the child's individuality and uniqueness. Knowing that a child has autism and how his difficulties are likely to impact upon his behaviour is undoubtedly important. However, assuming that a child will automatically behave in a particular way, and that little can be done about this, is unhelpful. With the support of their parents and practitioners in their education setting, all children can make positive changes to their behaviour. The challenge for practitioners is to 'set the scene' to minimise the negative impact of the child's condition upon his behaviour.

Children with autism

Autism covers a wide spectrum of difficulties, hence the term 'autistic spectrum disorder' which is commonly used to describe children with such difficulties. Children with severe autism are still educated almost exclusively in specialist settings and schools, but children at the less severe end of the spectrum, including those with Asperger's Syndrome, are increasingly found in mainstream settings. In the absence of a diagnosis, practitioners may still suspect that a particular child may be 'on the spectrum'. They should be wary of sharing such thoughts with parents; setting staff are not qualified to diagnose autism and could very easily alarm or offend parents. Practitioners can still discuss concerns with parents, focusing on areas of particular difficulty or need, without speculating as to whether the child might be autistic. If a child has difficulties similar to those found in a child with autism, similar strategies and interventions can be used. A diagnosis of autism is not needed to use a particular strategy!

Children with autism have difficulties in three main areas. These are:

◆ communication
◆ social interaction
◆ imagination.

Other common difficulties include:

◆ oversensitivity to sensory stimuli (e.g. particular sounds, textures or smells)
◆ obsessive or repetitive behaviour
◆ resistance to change
◆ an apparent lack of awareness of danger.

How might autism impact upon the child's behaviour?

◆ Limited attention and listening skills may mean that the child is frequently off-task and appearing to ignore requests and instructions.
◆ Difficulty understanding and following instructions may also be interpreted as wilful defiance.
◆ Difficulties with empathising, sharing, turn-taking and generally 'getting on' with other children may lead to the child being perceived as antisocial, uncaring and generally 'difficult'.
◆ Distress resulting from an unpredictable environment or a new or unexpected activity or event may lead to behaviours such as screaming, rocking and hand flapping.
◆ Distress resulting from sensory 'overload' (e.g. flashing lights, loud noises) may also lead to the above behaviours.
◆ Insistence on doing things in a particular way can easily be interpreted as stubbornness.

Early years practitioners should gather as much information as possible about how the child's autism affects their behaviour during the home or setting visit, so that they are well prepared before the child starts in the setting. A setting visit (or a series of such visits) is particularly valuable for children with autism, so that they are able to familiarise themselves with the setting in preparation for their entry. If the setting does not already have one, it is strongly recommended that staff try to make a photo book or video about the setting that the child and his family can borrow.

As well as talking to parents, practitioners should obviously make use of any available information from other professionals who have been involved with the child. Settings should try to arrange training on autism for all staff, but if this is not possible, the child's keyworker at least should be able to access relevant training. This may be available through the Local Education Authority.

Ideally, any necessary resources should be prepared before the child starts in the setting. A visual timetable (as described in Chapter 2) is particularly helpful in creating the predictable environment that most children with autism need. If the child has a speech and language therapist who has recommended the use of PECS (Picture Exchange Communication System), the therapist or a specialist teacher should be able to provide training and supervision to setting staff in the correct use of this approach. As well as giving the child a way of communicating effectively, PECS can be a particularly useful way of helping the child to feel less frustrated and more in control of his environment, leading to more positive behaviour. It is important that staff using PECS have been properly trained, as the system needs to be used in a very prescriptive way in order to be fully effective.

When a child with autism behaves in an unwanted way and the practitioner has no idea why, the ABC approach described in Chapter 6 should be used to try and identify the antecedents and consequences of the unwanted behaviour. It may sometimes appear that children with autism are behaving in bizarre and random ways, but practitioners should remember that any behaviour always happens for a reason and serves a particular purpose. Most behaviour issues in young children with autism are a result of communication difficulties, and it is therefore important that practitioners think about how autistic children can be taught to communicate in more appropriate ways. If practitioners are able to identify the antecedents to the behaviour, they can then look to change these to address the unwanted behaviour. As with any other child, strategies used should focus on rewarding the child for positive behaviour rather than imposing sanctions for unwanted behaviour. Consistency between all members of staff and perseverance are also vital.

Using social stories

Gray (2002) describes the use of social stories to help children with autism understand specific social situations and how to deal with them. The social story tells the child how he should behave when faced with a particular event or situation. Social stories work best for children who are able to understand simple sentences, but pictures, symbols and photographs can be used to illustrate the social story and help the child understand the given situation and what he should do.

A social story is made up of three types of sentence:

◆ descriptive – what is happening or what is going to happen and why
◆ perspective – a description of how people feel and react to a given situation
◆ directive – a description of what the child should do in a given situation.

The case study below illustrates the use of a social story in a reception class:

Case study: A social story to help Reece cope with lunchtimes

Reece was a 5-year-old boy who had recently been diagnosed with mild autism. He was making good progress in the reception class at his local primary school. However, he found transitions particularly difficult, and in particular became very distressed when he was told it was lunchtime. He hated washing his hands with the other children before lunch, and then became very upset if he saw that one of the foods on offer was something he did not like. He found it difficult to cope if it was noisy at lunchtime, and covered his ears with his hands, rocking backwards and forwards and making a moaning noise.

This is Reece's social story. It was made into a book and illustrated with photographs:

> 'Every day in school we have lunch.
> A grown-up will tell me it's nearly lunchtime and let me have the sand timer so I can see when it's time to wash my hands.
> I can wash my hands before the other children, before it gets too noisy in the bathroom.
> After I've washed my hands, I will sit at the table for lunch.
> A grown up will ask me what I would like to eat.
> I can choose what I would like to eat.
> Most people have foods they don't like.
> It doesn't matter if I don't like something; I don't have to have it on my plate and I don't have to eat it.
> If it gets too noisy, I can say "Shhh!" and a grown-up will ask the children to be quieter.
> If I get too upset, I can go and sit on the carpet.'

Following the introduction of the social story, Reece was much less upset at the prospect of lunchtime, and by the end of the term, this was one of his favourite times of the day.

More strategies for promoting positive behaviour in young autistic children

◆ Practitioners should try to ensure routine, structure and predictability through the setting day. Photographs, symbols, visual timetables and social stories can all be used to help with this.

◆ Practitioners should watch for children who subtly annoy the child with autism and position them away from him if possible.

◆ Practitioners should be aware that the child may be defensive of his own personal space, and try to anticipate and act before difficulties arise.

◆ Practitioners could collect some of the child's favourite things together in a special box. These can then be used to distract the child when something is upsetting him.

◆ Practitioners could try talking or drawing through stressful situations or should remove the child from the stressful situation.

◆ Practitioners should make sure that there is a safe place that the child can retreat to when he gets angry or upset.

◆ Practitioners can use the child's obsessions as rewards. For example, if a child is obsessed with dinosaurs, staff should let him know that he will be allowed to play with the dinosaurs after he has done something of their choosing or behaved in a particular way.

◆ Practitioners could set themselves the challenge of finding new ways of engaging the child in his obsession or particular interest. Rather than simply letting the child play with toy dinosaurs for extended periods, could they engage him in making dinosaur-shaped biscuits or constructing a giant dinosaur from cardboard boxes in the outdoor area? Such activities could also provide opportunities for developing social skills such as turn-taking and cooperative working.

◆ Like all children, children with autism need clear boundaries that are consistently applied by all members of staff.

◆ Practitioners should ensure that children understand *why* their behaviour is unacceptable. The practitioner should state the rule and how the child needs to behave to abide by it.

◆ Practitioners should consider whether the obsession, routine or repetitive behaviour restricts the child's opportunities, causes distress or discomfort or impacts on his learning. If not, is it really necessary to stop it? Practitioners should focus their efforts on developing positive behaviour strategies that concentrate on clearly unacceptable behaviour rather than that which is merely 'odd' or unusual.

◆ Where it is necessary to limit obsessions, routines or repetitive behaviours, practitioners can set limits in a range of ways:
  – limit the object (e.g. the child is only allowed to bring one dinosaur to nursery)
  – limit the time (e.g. the child can only play with dinosaurs for half an hour at a time)
  – limit the place (e.g. the child can only play with dinosaurs in a designated part of the nursery).

◆ Limits need to be set using clear rules which state where, when, with whom or for how long the behaviour is allowed to occur. Practitioners should present this information visually to support the child's understanding and to help him cope with any anxiety that restricted access to the obsession or activity may create.

◆ Practitioners should interrupt repetitive behaviours by redirecting the child to another enjoyable and appropriate activity that serves the same purpose as the repetitive behaviour. For example, the practitioner could redirect a child who is rocking for sensory input to a swing or rocking toy.

◆ Practitioners should aim to make use of children's obsessions in order to develop their skills and interests. Practitioners should think creatively about a particular obsession and try to come up with ways of developing it into a more functional activity for the child. For example, an obsession tearing paper could be developed into making papier mâché.

◆ Practitioners could consider implementing a buddy system, whereby the child's peers help to support a child with autism. Children are asked to volunteer to be 'buddies' every day (to avoid the same few children being overburdened). Staff need to explain to the children what the role entails and how to seek adult support where needed. The 'buddies' agree to play with the child and to help him manage tasks and routines in the setting.

Further information on working with young children with autism is available from the National Autistic Society, 393 City Road, London EC1V 1NG. The society's website has lots of useful information and resources: www.nas.org.uk.

Children with attention difficulties/ADD/ADHD

All young children are likely to have difficulty paying attention from time to time. Children in the early years naturally tend to have quite short attention spans. It could be argued that the more exciting practitioners are able to make the learning environment, the more children will be able to sustain their attention and concentration. While this is likely to be true for most children, it is important to be aware that a very exciting and stimulating environment might also result in a child who is prone to hyperactivity going into 'overdrive'. Practitioners will need to consider strategies for helping children to calm down when they become overexcited.

Some young children will find it particularly difficult to attend and to sustain focus and concentration, and some of these children may have a diagnosis of Attention Deficit Hyperactivity Disorder (ADHD). This condition is characterised by difficulties in three main areas:

◆ hyperactivity
◆ impulsivity
◆ difficulty in paying attention and concentrating.

The exact cause of ADHD is unknown, but it is clear that genetic (inherited) factors play a part. Studies using brain scanning techniques have found that children with severe symptoms of ADHD have lower than normal activity in the parts of the brain involved in planning activity, controlling impulses, controlling movements and sustaining attention. It is clear that the environment also plays a part in ADHD, but no one is to 'blame' for this condition; there is no evidence to suggest that parental behaviour or the way in which a child is brought up can cause ADHD.

There is no medical test for ADHD – diagnosis follows careful observation of the child and discussion with parents and others. In order for a child to receive a diagnosis of ADHD, the difficulties need to be apparent in different settings (e.g. at home as well as in the child's nursery) and will probably be evident by the time the child enters their first education setting.

The term Attention Deficit Disorder (ADD) may be used to describe children who have difficulties with attention and concentration but are not necessarily hyperactive or impulsive. There is a risk that such children's difficulties may go unnoticed for some time as it is the hyperactivity that tends to make children with ADHD immediately stand out. For ease of reading, from this point forward the term ADHD will be used throughout this section of the chapter when discussing children with attention difficulties, whether or not the child is hyperactive or has a formal diagnosis. As with other conditions, a diagnosis is not needed for the practitioner to use the suggested interventions. The same strategies work equally well for all children with attention difficulties, whether or not they have a diagnosis of ADHD. Practitioners should focus less on the label and more on positive strategies for helping all children in the setting to improve their attention and concentration skills.

How might ADHD impact upon the child's behaviour?

◆ A child with ADHD might race around the setting, be unable to sit still, and interfere with other children's activities. Such behaviour is likely to be unpopular with peers, and the child may be seen as 'naughty'.

◆ Frustration resulting from rejection may lead to further unwanted behaviour.

◆ The child's difficulties in waiting may mean that he calls out answers to questions, and 'pushes in' when required to wait for a turn. These behaviours may further increase his unpopularity among his peers.

◆ The child may become distressed, because he does not want to behave inappropriately in the setting, yet does not know how to change.

◆ Attention and concentration difficulties mean that the child with ADHD tends to find it difficult to learn new skills. As a result, the child is at risk of underachieving, and may 'act up' to mask his difficulties.

◆ A child with ADHD may not realise how his behaviour impacts on other people. His immature social skills mean that he may not know how to make friends or to sustain relationships. If this is the case, the child may become isolated and socially withdrawn.

Early years practitioners will need to keep a very close eye on children with these sorts of difficulties to ensure that appropriate action is taken to minimise the negative impact. Fortunately, there are many useful strategies that practitioners can employ to support the child with ADHD. If the child's early years in education can be made as positive as possible, there is a good chance that he will learn to deal with his difficulties in a more constructive manner, paving the way for more positive behaviour and academic progress in his future schooling.

Strategies for promoting positive behaviour in young children with ADHD

◆ Practitioners should say the child's name to attract his attention and ensure that eye contact is made before speaking to him. If the child has difficulty maintaining eye contact, practitioners can place a small, interesting object (such as a brightly coloured marble) on the child's nose and then move it towards their own nose. This unusual-sounding strategy often works well.

◆ Practitioners should encourage the child to repeat what they have said in his own words to check that he has heard and understood. A good way of doing this is to ask the child to tell the other children: 'John, can you tell the group what they have to do?'

◆ When speaking to the child, practitioners should keep sentences short and simple. Instructions should be broken down into small steps so that the child only has one thing to remember at once.

◆ Like children with autism, children with ADHD respond well to structure, routine and a predictable environment. Practitioners should make use of visual timetables and other visual cues to support the child's memory and understanding.

◆ Practitioners should encourage the child with ADHD to sit at the front next to them during carpet sessions. The child should also be seated away from windows, doorways and other potential distractions. When the child is on the carpet, practitioners should aim to interact with him frequently (e.g. asking questions, inviting comments) to maintain his attention. Practitioners should aim to surround the child with good role models while on the carpet.

◆ Practitioners should ensure that activities requiring high levels of concentration are appropriately supported and alternated with less intense activities. The child with ADHD should be encouraged to return to activities he has abandoned later in the day. Staff should encourage the child to feel comfortable with seeking help.

◆ Practitioners should make sure that targets set are short and achievable and that the child is praised immediately upon completion of the task.

◆ Practitioners should give the child with ADHD extra time for certain tasks, but must not penalise him for needing extra time. The child should never miss out on a fun activity or treat because he is finishing another task.

◆ Where children are required to wait for a turn, practitioners should allow the child with ADHD to be among the first to be chosen. As the child becomes more able to wait, his turn can be delayed slightly.

◆ Practitioners should ask themselves whether it is really necessary for children to line up. If it is, they could try giving the child with ADHD a special object to play with while lining up, such as a stop watch. This object should only be used while lining up, so that it effectively functions as a transitional object, cueing the child that a new activity is coming up. Practitioners may worry that the other children will see this as somehow unfair, but in fact children are usually very understanding if the practitioner takes time to explain to them why the child with ADHD needs this object.

◆ Rather than frequently having to ask the child to change his behaviour (e.g. 'stop interrupting'; 'stop pushing'; 'stop running'), the practitioner could decide a 'secret signal' with the child to remind him when he needs to change his behaviour. This avoids drawing excessive attention to the child with ADHD.

◆ Practitioners should avoid or limit competitive activities, as these may cause the child with ADHD to act aggressively. Instead, practitioners should focus on cooperative activities that will help the child to learn appropriate social interaction skills. It is important that a high level of adult supervision is given during such activities, as the child with ADHD is likely to need support until he has learnt how to work and play cooperatively.

◆ Practitioners should ensure that the child with ADHD has enough physical outlets for his energy throughout the day. Think about opportunities indoors (e.g. playing drums) as well as outdoors.

- Children with ADHD often respond well to being given errands to run or special responsibilities. This has the added benefit of allowing their peers to see them in a more positive light.
- Practitioners should encourage parents to introduce clear routines at home (e.g. mealtimes and bedtimes at the same time each day). This will help the child to follow routines in the setting.
- Practitioners should teach the child to reward himself. They should promote positive self-talk (e.g. 'You did really well staying in your seat today! How do you feel about that?') This encourages the children to think positively of themselves.

Children who are withdrawn or very distressed

When thinking about young children's behaviour, most early years practitioners will naturally focus upon those behaviours they find most challenging, such as defiance, aggressiveness and destructiveness. However, it is important that children who display withdrawn or distressed behaviour are not forgotten, as these children are also in need of practitioners' attention and support. Such children may easily 'fall through the net' because their behaviour tends not to cause a problem for anyone else in the setting. Even very distressed children may not always show obvious outward signs of their distress such as crying. In contrast, it is difficult to ignore the child who is attention seeking or challenging of adults' authority.

Children may be withdrawn for a number of reasons. Clearly, there is a great deal of natural variation in children's level of sociability and some children may be naturally shy and introverted. At what point does natural shyness become 'withdrawal'? Practitioners need not be overly concerned with the terms used to describe these children, but should instead ask themselves: 'Is this child so withdrawn that it is having a negative impact upon her happiness and achievement?' If the answer to this question is yes, then the practitioner needs to think carefully about how best to support such children to enable them to overcome their difficulties.

Similarly, children may be distressed, depressed or otherwise emotionally vulnerable for a number of reasons. Of course, all children will be distressed from time to time, but generally recover from their distress remarkably quickly. If a child is very distressed for a significant proportion of the day, on a regular basis, and is difficult to console, then this is clearly cause for concern. The probable reason for the child's distress may be known to the practitioner (e.g. bereavement, family illness or a difficult divorce) or may be unknown. The child's distress may be communicated via:

- recurrent crying
- elective mutism (choosing not to talk)
- frequent wetting/bedwetting or soiling after the child is toilet-trained
- very withdrawn behaviour
- aggressive behaviour
- self-harm
- excessive attention-seeking behaviour.

Whatever the reason for a child's withdrawn or distressed behaviour, there is much that practitioners can do to support such children. The starting point should always be a sensitive discussion with the child's parents to find out if there are any underlying reasons for the child's behaviour, such as a family bereavement. If a child who has previously been happy and sociable in her setting suddenly becomes withdrawn or very distressed, it is likely that a particular event, either at home or in the setting, has triggered this response. When discussing concerns with parents, it is very important that practitioners do not inadvertently give parents the impression that they are somehow to blame for their child's emotional difficulties. An acrimonious divorce, for example, is likely to take its toll on a child, but the last thing parents need at a time of enormous upheaval and stress is to feel guilty that they are in some way 'damaging' their child through their decision to divorce.

Strategies for promoting positive behaviour in withdrawn and very distressed children

- Practitioners should consider setting up a nurture corner as described in Chapter 3, and ensure that this area of the setting is appropriately supported by staff.
- Practitioners should aim to provide a friendly, secure environment. Ideally, shouting and loud noises should be kept to a minimum, although it is appreciated that this is not always easy in early years settings.
- Practitioners should keep a close eye on withdrawn children to make sure that they are not being picked on by other children, as they can easily be targeted by their peers.
- Practitioners should give lots of hugs and cuddles to children who like to receive them. However, some withdrawn and distressed children do not like close physical contact. Practitioners should take their lead from children in this area, responding to requests (both overt and non-verbal) for hugs/cuddles, rather than 'imposing' them.
- Practitioners should allow children to keep a comforter, if they appear to need this.
- Practitioners should encourage children to talk about their feelings, but also respect children's wishes if they do not wish to discuss feelings.
- Practitioners should never make the child join in with whole-group activities if she does not wish to do so.
- Practitioners may wish to consider allocating a 'buddy' to the withdrawn child. A good 'buddy' would be socially skilled, but not the most extrovert child in the group, as this may be difficult for the withdrawn child to deal with.
- In many cases, withdrawn children may have a comparatively good relationship with one particular member of staff. Settings should wherever possible allocate the child's trusted adult as her keyworker.
- Practitioners should be sensitive in their choice of storybooks. For example, if a child's parent is in prison, it would be wise to avoid stories about 'cops and robbers'.
- Where a child has experienced a bereavement, it may be appropriate for practitioners to talk to the child's peers (when the bereaved child is not present), to provide opportunities for them to ask questions and discuss how they can

support the child. The child's peers can be encouraged to acknowledge her loss, for example to say, 'I'm sorry your Daddy died'.

◆ Practitioners should give bereaved children the opportunity to talk privately about their loss. Even if the child cannot verbalise her feelings, it is helpful for a trusted practitioner to show sympathy (avoiding comments such as 'I know how you feel') and to use words like *sad, lonely, upset* and *scared*, so that the child realises that the setting knows about the death and acknowledges her feelings.

◆ With parents' permission, practitioners should seek support from other relevant professionals if the child's difficulties persist or if her emotional state deteriorates further.

Chapter 9

Making positive links

To conclude the book, this chapter focuses upon sources of support for positive intervention in children's behaviour and highlights the importance of making arrangements for a positive transition to the child's next setting.

Involving external professionals

For the vast majority of children, practitioners will be able to use the positive behaviour strategies outlined in this book without needing to involve external professionals. However, it is recognised that for a small number of children, the support of outside professionals may be beneficial. Children who are excessively aggressive or destructive, those with diagnosed conditions such as autism or ADHD and those showing signs of severe depression or displaying self-injurious behaviours are among those for whom external support is likely to be needed.

In line with the Special Educational Needs Code of Practice (DfES, 2001), external professionals are involved at the 'Early Years Action Plus' stage of intervention. This means that settings will already have implemented strategies that are additional to or different from those usually provided in the setting in order to support the child's behaviour ('Early Years Action'). The child will have had an Individual Education Plan (IEP) outlining the behaviour targets set and the strategies to be used in working towards these targets. If, following a review of the child's progress, s/he is considered to have made only very limited progress towards the targets set, a decision may be made to seek the support of external professionals or support services.

At every stage of the Code of Practice, it is vital that parents' views are sought and taken account of, and that they are fully informed about what is being done to support their child's behaviour. Obviously, parental permission must be sought before moving a child between stages of the Code of Practice, and parents must give their informed consent in order for external professionals and agencies to be involved. For consent to be 'informed', parents must have been told:

◆ who would be involved (including their full name)
◆ this professional's job title

◆ the agency or service for whom the professional works
◆ the exact role of the professional
◆ the form that the professional's involvement would take (e.g. observation, consultation with setting staff, direct work with child)
◆ why the professional's involvement is thought to be appropriate.

In addition, parents should be given the opportunity to ask any questions they may have about the professional and his or her involvement. Parents must be made aware that they are at liberty to decline the professional's involvement, and practitioners should not place inappropriate pressure upon parents to consent to this involvement. In the majority of cases, parents are likely to view the professional's involvement in a positive light. However, if parents are anxious or concerned about the prospect of external professional involvement, practitioners should make every effort to reassure them and allay any fears they may have. This highlights the importance of settings having built a trusting and mutually supportive relationship with parents. If this has been achieved, parents are much more likely to see external involvement as a positive intervention which is in their child's best interests, and not as an opportunity for their child to be labelled as a 'problem'.

Professionals who may be involved

The educational psychologist

As the name suggests, educational psychologists (EPs) are fully qualified psychologists who receive specialised training in the application of psychology to educational issues. They provide assessment of and advice about children's individual needs, including their behaviour. Most EPs are employed by local education authorities (LEAs), usually as part of the LEA's Educational Psychology Service, but a few are now employed by Early Years Services.

For early years practitioners based in maintained schools, access to an EP is usually via the school's Special Educational Needs Co-ordinator[1] (SENCO) who prioritises children to be seen by the EP. In most LEAs, schools have an allocated number of EP visits per year. In some areas, schools 'buy in' to the EP service, and can choose how many visits to purchase. A minority of LEAs may still have a system whereby referrals are made centrally to the Educational Psychology Service and then allocated to EPs on a case-by-case basis. Whichever system is in place, practitioners in schools should speak to the SENCO if they wish to refer a child in their class to the EP. The SENCO is often the member of staff who discusses the proposed referral with parents. However, for children in the early years, where there is hopefully a close and trusting relationship between parents and practitioners, it may be more appropriate for a member of staff from the child's class to discuss the referral and request consent.

Non-maintained early years settings (e.g. playgroups and private or voluntary nurseries) may not have allocated visits from an EP, as most Educational

1 In some schools and settings, the term Inclusion Co-ordinator may be used in preference to SENCO. This reflects the school's commitment to inclusion and the recognition that all children have individual needs, not only those with the 'SEN' label.

Psychology Services do not have the capacity to provide a time allocation service to these settings. However, even if this is the case, it may be worthwhile for the practitioner to contact their LEA's Educational Psychology Service for advice. Even if the service is unable to provide an assessment, it should still be able to advise settings on alternative sources of support. Where the LEA has agreed to carry out a statutory assessment of a child's needs, an EP must contribute towards this assessment, and will almost certainly wish to visit the child in his educational setting as part of the assessment. If this is the case, practitioners should make the most of the EP's visit and ensure that they have the opportunity to discuss relevant issues and get advice from the EP about positive behaviour intervention strategies.

The Area SENCO

Since 2001, Local Education Authorities in the UK have been introducing Area SENCOs[2] as a resource to support the government's manifesto commitment that children with special educational needs should have their needs identified earlier. Area SENCOs are employed to work with staff in non-maintained settings, recognising that these settings have until recently had very little support in comparison with maintained schools. The role of the Area SENCO is to support and empower staff in early years settings to enable them to develop inclusive early learning environments and to provide support in identifying individual needs and removing barriers to learning.

Area SENCOs should have experience of working with children for whom behaviour has been raised as a concern. They should be able to give staff further ideas for positive behaviour management strategies and also be able to provide (or arrange) training for staff that focuses upon young children's behaviour. Area SENCOs may also be able to give advice to parents about their child's behaviour, and should be aware of further sources of support available to settings within the local area.

The Child and Family Consultation Service

Health Authorities provide a Child and Family Consultation Service (or something similar) as part of their range of Child and Adolescent Mental Health Services (CAMHS). The aims of such a service are:

◆ to prevent children's mental health difficulties from escalating;
◆ to help and improve serious problems, disorders and mental illnesses.

Child and Family Consultation Services are staffed by psychiatrists, psychologists, psychotherapists, social workers and mental health nurses. These professionals often work in multi-disciplinary teams, so that they can share all their knowledge and skills to understand and help children and families experiencing difficulties. Where a child's behaviour is of great concern at home as well as in their early

2 The exact job title may vary. Other variations currently in use include Area Inclusion Co-ordinator and Early Years SEN Officer.

years setting, practitioners may wish to suggest that parents consider a referral to the local Child and Family Consultation Service. Such a suggestion needs to be made sensitively, with professionals using their professional judgement as to whether the suggestion would be well received. Settings may wish to ask another professional such as their Area SENCO to discuss this option with parents.

Children visiting a Child and Family Consultation Service will often be accompanied by other family members, as the service aims to understand children's behaviour in the context of their family and to mobilise the family's resources to help the child. The staff at the Child and Family Consultation Service will also be interested in children's behaviour and relationships within their early years setting. With appropriate support, the child's behaviour will hopefully begin to improve both at home and in the setting. Parents may wish to share the strategies suggested by the Child and Family Consultation Service with setting staff, and this is obviously to be encouraged. It could potentially be very productive for setting staff to share information with the Child and Family Consultation Service, but this should only take place with the consent and blessing of the child's family. Practitioners should avoid asking parents potentially intrusive questions about what happens during appointments, as much of this information may be very personal to the family.

The specialist teacher

Most Local Education Authorities employ teams of specialist teachers who have expertise in particular areas such as sensory impairment, learning difficulties or behaviour. These teams are usually centrally based within the LEA and the specialist teachers visit schools and settings in order to advise staff of how best to meet the child's needs. The specialist teachers for behaviour within an LEA may work exclusively with maintained schools or may also work in non-maintained early years settings. Practitioners who feel that they would benefit from the advice and support of a specialist teacher for behaviour should contact the LEA in order to check whether they are able to access this service. It may also be possible to arrange this service through the setting's Area SENCO.

Transition to the child's next setting

As the time approaches for children to move on to their next setting, it is important that practitioners consider the arrangements that need to be made to ensure a positive transition. Many settings already have excellent practice in this area, but there are still those who make few, if any, links with receiving schools. A properly planned transition is beneficial to all children, but it is particularly important for those for whom behaviour has been a concern.

For children in nursery and reception classes in schools, the transition will be within the same building, which provides some degree of continuity for the child. Children will move with their peers into the new class and are likely to know their new teacher at least by sight. It is a good idea for children to visit their next class in the summer term before they leave their early years class. This will provide an opportunity for children to meet their next teacher and to familiarise themselves with a different classroom. During such visits, it is not helpful for the receiving teacher to make comments such as 'I've heard all about you – I'll be keeping my eye on you!' Although such comments may be meant light-heartedly, they send a powerful message to children that they are 'known about' and that they cannot be expected or trusted to behave positively. All children deserve a 'fresh start' in their new class, including those for whom behaviour has been an issue.

The practitioners in the child's early years class should find time to meet with the receiving teacher and any support staff to share information and discuss progress. At this point, it is useful to share positive behaviour strategies that have worked well for the child, as well as any areas of particular difficulty. It is important that staff present a balanced picture of the child, focusing on strengths and not only difficulties.

Where children are moving from a non-maintained early years setting into school, transition is likely to be a much more complex process, and is undoubtedly a major upheaval for the child. Whether this is a positive upheaval or a negative upheaval will depend to a large extent upon the effectiveness of the arrangements made for transition.

Hopefully, parents will have obtained a place for their child in a school of their choice well in advance of the child's departure from the early years setting. This allows time for a transition meeting to be set up between the current setting and the receiving school. Unless the two establishments already have a good working relationship, or the LEA has clear guidelines for transition, it will be unclear who should 'make the first move'. Early years practitioners in non-maintained settings may feel nervous about contacting school staff, and school staff may not think to contact practitioners in the child's early years setting. It is strongly recommended that all early years settings have a transition policy that includes details of how links are made with receiving schools. It may be possible to involve a member of staff from the LEA Early Years Service to offer support in writing such a policy and to act as a point of contact between settings and schools.

Assuming that it has been possible to arrange a transition meeting, this would ideally be attended by the child's parents and any external professionals who had been involved with the child, in addition to staff from both the setting and school. Children's behaviour should be discussed in the context of their overall progress, and, as said before, staff should remember to give due weight to the child's strengths and positive behaviours. Positive behaviour strategies should be shared, and, with parents' permission, relevant records should be passed to the receiving setting. It is particularly helpful if two-way visits can be arranged whereby the school staff visit children in their early years setting, while setting staff accompany children on a visit to their new school.

If children are likely to need additional support in their new school (e.g. if they have a statement of special educational needs), this should be arranged before the child starts, so that the support is in place right from the start. Children who have difficulties with their behaviour may find the transition to school particularly challenging, and it is important to try to ensure that the first few days are as positive as possible. Where early years practitioners have worked hard to ensure that the child's behaviour is as positive as possible, it would be a great shame if behaviour were to deteriorate due to a poorly planned transition.

Appendix I

Behaviour audit form for early years settings

This proforma is designed to assist settings in thinking about their approach to children's behaviour. It may help settings to identify areas in which changes may be made to support more positive behaviour in young children.

Questions for practitioners to consider:	Yes/No	Any action to be taken:
Does the setting have a positive behaviour policy? If so, have all staff had the opportunity to contribute to this? Were parents consulted?		
Do staff gather appropriate information from parents (e.g. significant early experiences; behaviour strategies used at home) before their children start in the setting?		
Are parents who express concerns about their child's behaviour reassured that staff will work in partnership with them to promote positive behaviour?		
Do staff make appropriate arrangements for settling new children (e.g. staggering entry; preparing the room; encouraging parents to stay)?		

Questions for practitioners to consider:	Yes/ No	Any action to be taken:
Do staff provide an appropriate balance of adult-led and child-initiated activities?		
Do children have free access to the outdoor area?		
Are occasions on which children are expected to wait kept to a minimum?		
Do practitioners place pressure upon children to take part in particular activities, or are children free to decide not to participate?		
Are activities explained appropriately, at a level children can understand, so that they know what is expected of them and how to carry out the activity?		
Do staff allow children to abandon activities when they have lost interest and encourage them to return to the activity later?		
Can children immediately begin an activity when they arrive in the setting?		
Do staff prepare children for transitions and give them warning when activities are about to end?		
Do the setting's arrangements for drink, snack and mealtimes promote positive behaviour?		
Do staff allow children to engage in superhero play without constantly intervening?		
Do staff offer children appropriate support to complete structured tasks, without doing the task for the child?		
Are children taught to deal with unexpected events?		

Questions for practitioners to consider:	Yes/ No	Any action to be taken:
Is a visual timetable used to support children's understanding of the routine of the setting day?		
Do staff give children regular praise, always aiming to 'catch the child being good'?		
Do staff ignore low-level inappropriate behaviours wherever possible?		
Does the layout of the room(s) promote positive behaviour (e.g. is there enough space for children to move around freely without bumping into each other?)?		
Do staff use a 'thinking chair' or an alternative strategy to give children 'time-out' to think about their behaviour?		
Are effective arrangements in place to support children who are angry or upset?		
Do staff feel confident that they are able to deal with violent or destructive outbursts in as positive a way as possible?		
Have staff thought about any particular issues involved in promoting positive behaviour outdoors (e.g. how to ensure that boys do not dominate bikes or other equipment)?		
Is ICT used to support children's behaviour in the setting?		
Is music used to support children's behaviour in the setting?		
Are staff clear about what constitutes unacceptable behaviour for the setting, and why?		

Questions for practitioners to consider:	Yes/ No	Any action to be taken:
Does the setting have clear rules that are positively worded and discussed with the children on a regular basis?		
Do all staff have the same expectations of children's behaviour and are strategies, rewards and sanctions applied consistently by all members of the team?		
Do staff take care not to stereotype children by gender, ethnicity or any other attribute?		
Do staff respond to children's individual learning styles and interests?		
Do staff make appropriate use of props and other visual cues to support children's understanding?		
Do staff promote children's emotional literacy, and give thought to their own emotional needs?		
Do staff teach children appropriate strategies to manage and express anger?		
Are staff clear about why they observe children?		
Do staff focus upon the positive as well as the unwanted behaviour when observing children?		
Do staff think about the antecedents and consequences to children's behaviour?		
Do staff engage in joint problem solving to try to minimise unwanted behaviour?		
Do staff objectively record children's behaviour rather than their own interpretation of that behaviour?		

Questions for practitioners to consider:	Yes/No	Any action to be taken:
Do staff record positive behaviour at least as often as they record unwanted behaviour?		
Are all staff committed to working in partnership with parents?		
Are parents made aware of their rights and responsibilities in relation to their children's behaviour, and are they aware of staff's rights and responsibilities?		
Do staff make time to meet with parents, including those who work full-time?		
Do staff discuss children's behaviour with parents in a positive and constructive way?		
Do staff respond appropriately to parents' requests for help?		
Do staff take account of possible cultural differences in child-rearing practice and avoid making negative judgements about parents' methods?		
Are parents encouraged to volunteer in the setting, and are they properly inducted in how to do this (e.g. how to respond if their own child 'acts out')?		
Would all staff be committed to including children who have conditions such as autism or ADHD?		
Does the setting know how to access training and support when working with children with such conditions?		
Do staff watch out for withdrawn or distressed children, and offer them appropriate support?		

Questions for practitioners to consider:	Yes/ No	Any action to be taken:
Do staff seek support from outside professionals when needed, and do they implement the strategies suggested by these professionals?		
Does the setting have a transition policy?		

Behaviour recording form

Antecedents (triggers to the behaviour) Think about: ◆ *when* the behaviour happened ◆ *where* the child was ◆ *who* the child was with ◆ *what* the child was doing	
Behaviour Describe this clearly and objectively, avoiding interpretation at this point.	
Consequences What happens as a result of the child's behaviour? What are the child's aims? How do adults and other children respond to the behaviour?	

How can antecedents be changed, if necessary, to promote more positive behaviour?

Can the consequences of the behaviour be changed to make positive behaviour more likely?

What rewards does the child enjoy?

Sample behaviour section from a home–setting agreement

N.B. This is provided as an example to give some indication of what might be included in the behaviour section of a home–setting agreement. It is important that settings develop their own agreements, in their own words, consulting with parents and all members of staff. A complete home–setting agreement would also have other sections, including children's learning.

The setting agrees to:	I/We, . . .'s parent(s), agree to:
Inform both children and parents of the setting's rules and explain why these are important.	Encourage my/our child to follow the setting's rules.
Establish clear, consistent and fair boundaries for children's behaviour in the setting.	Encourage my/our child to behave appropriately in the setting and at home.
Treat all children fairly in dealing with their behaviour.	Encourage my/our child to tell an adult when another child has hurt them, instead of hurting the child back.
Speak to children calmly and politely, avoiding shouting, sarcasm or humiliation.	Speak to staff calmly and politely.
Praise children when they are behaving as wanted.	Talk to my/our child about their good behaviour in the setting.
Implement a system that focuses upon children earning rewards for positive behaviour rather than being sanctioned for unwanted behaviour.	Reinforce the system used in the setting at home.

The setting agrees to:	*I/We, . . .'s parent(s), agree to:*
Let parents know about any incidents or concerns as soon as they arise.	1. Let staff know about any home factors that may be influencing my/our child's behaviour.
	2. Not punish my/our child for behaviour that has already been dealt with in the setting.
Speak to the parents of other children about incidents where necessary.	Not ask staff or my/our child to point out another child who was involved in an incident with them.
Listen to parents' thoughts and concerns and let them know what action staff will take in response.	Listen to staff's thoughts and concerns.
Admit when mistakes have been made and apologise.	Admit when mistakes have been made and apologise.

References

Brooker, L. (2002) *Starting School – Young Children and Learning Cultures*, Maidenhead: Open University Press.

Chafin, S., Roy, M., Gerin, W. and Christenfeld, N. (2004) 'Music can facilitate blood pressure recovery from stress', *British Journal of Health Psychology*, 9: 393–403.

Desforges, C. and Abouchaar, A. (2003) *The Impact of Parental Involvement, Parental Support and Family Education on Pupil Achievement and Adjustment: A Review of Literature*, Nottingham: DfES.

DfES (2001) *Special Educational Needs Code of Practice*, Annesley: DfES.

Gray, C. (2002) *My Social Stories Book*, London: Jessica Kingsley Publishers.

Holloway, L. (2004) Black Information Link: *Exclusions shake-up demanded*. Online. Available at http://www.blink.org.uk/pdescription.asp?key=4422&grp=7&cat=367 (accessed 12 June 2005).

Home Office (2003) *Respect and Responsibility: Taking a Stand Against Anti-Social Behaviour*, London: The Stationery Office.

LDA Education Commission (2004) *Rampton Revisited: The Educational Experiences and Achievements of Black Boys in London Schools 2000–2003*, London: London Development Agency.

Morgan, R. (2004) *Children's Views on Restraint*, Newcastle: Office of the Children's Rights Director.

Passey, D., Rogers, C., Machell, J. and McHugh, G. (2004) *The Motivational Effect of ICT on Pupils*, Annesley: DfES Publications.

Qualifications and Curriculum Authority (QCA) (2000) *Curriculum Guidance for the Foundation Stage*, London: QCA.

Sykes, G. (2001) 'Home School Agreements: a tool for parental control or for partnership?' *Educational Psychology in Practice*, 17(3): 273–286.

Index